There <u>IS</u> No Joy In
GRUNTSVILLE

But There's Plenty To Learn!

"Lessons to turn trials into triumphs: Grunts into rising stars"

by
Ron Hostetler and
Jeff Hostetler

NATIONAL FOOTBALL LEAGUE
All-Pro Quarterback
Superbowl XXV Champion

Foreword by
JIM TUNNEY, Ed.D., CSP, CPAE

ISBN: 0-937539-11-2

Table Of Contents

FOREWORD

The thing about Ron and Jeff Hostetler, the character trait that qualifies them to be our tour guides through the tough and trying times of Gruntsville, is their perseverance and stick-to-it work ethic. Their willingness to hold themselves accountable is what gives, and will always give them the focus to stay competitive in things that burn out most others within a few years. It's also what makes them leaders.

To understand the balance and perspective that underpins their competitive drive, it helps to look back on what was going on in the lives of these brothers and their family at home on the farm in Western Pennsylvania.

Both were natural athletes and into sports. As were their other two brothers, Doug and Todd. All were strong armed, Pennsylvania quarterbacks at Conemaugh Township High School, and great on both sides of the ball. All were scholar athletes, earning high honors both on and off the gridiron, basketball court, and baseball field. Jeff, by the way, distinguished himself further by becoming Valedictorian of his senior class.

Still, no one plays four sports and hits the books with such remarkably equal excellence without a willingness to make the time, and give the concentration, to overcome pressure and the inevitable setbacks. No one excels, not even with natural talent, without growing a good wide streak of resoluteness. And that's what Gruntsville is all about. Growing and reaping bold, firm and steady determination.

You might describe Ron and Jeff's pursuit of excellence as a sure sense of purpose joined with a sure sense of self. They can see themselves squarely–no pretense, no false hope–just plenty of good honest optimism grounded in the willingness to do the work and the mental toughness to treat the hard stuff as just part of it.

Out of Conemaugh Township High School, Jeff landed at Penn State on an athletic scholarship to work with the renowned, the legendary, Joe Paterno. He followed on the trail of his brother Ron, a highly recruited quarterback turned linebacker by Paterno, who became another of Penn State's famous linebackers drafted into the NFL after winning pre-season All-American and co-captain honors his senior year.

Like Ron, Jeff headed up to Happy Valley assured he could win the starting quarterback job with the Nittany Lions. He did, but after a year of always looking over his shoulder, he found himself on the outside looking in.

Rather than sitting the bench, or switching to linebacker like his brother, he opted to take what he had learned to West Virginia. He definitely found a better fit with Coach Nielen (I won't get into the serendipity of his later marrying the coach's daughter). He was at the top of his class again scholastically, and working up the field pretty good, too. He led West Virginia to 9-3 records in both years (junior and senior), was named ABC Player of the Week, All-American quarterback both years; elected Academic All-American as a senior, one of only eleven students nationwide honored by the National Football Foundation; *and* nominated for a Rhodes Scholarship.

Somehow the cavernous Meadowlands was more attractive to Jeff than the banks of the Thames along Oxford. With the Giants, under Bill Parcels, Jeff was held in reserve while Phil Simms was having his hey days (one of those days was taking the Giants to a win in Super Bowl XXI).

"You can," according to Yogi Barra, "Observe a lot just by watching." I'd add, you can if you pay attention, keep your eagerness honed, do the film studies, the physical training, the nutrition essentials, and, resolutely, stay ready. You will need a head and body full of mental toughness when you "get the call". The mental toughness–the willingness and readiness to commit and perform–has to be as strong as it would be if you had been out there every game, every play.

It's a whole lot easier to be out-there-in-the-action-ready than it is to be sideline-ready. Ask Steve Young, another quintessential backup quarterback. Young waited on the sideline in San Francisco while Joe Montana had everyone "hey-heying" longer than most guys have a seat on the bus. Put Young, Hostetler, Steve Deberg and Frank Reich in a room together and you would get a whole lot of truth about the will, the stamina, the purposeful patience it takes to wait and wait and wait, and stay ready, for years!

Still, when the call came, Hoss was ready. Simms went down with a broken leg in game 14 of the 1990 season. Hoss stepped in and directed the Giants to a pair of wins that clinched the NFC East title. He proceeded with three straight playoff victories culminating with a 20 for 32, 222-yard one-touchdown performance in the Super Bowl XXV victory over Buffalo. Now, that's what I call stepping forward when the call comes.

The records mounted. His interception percentage was an astonishing 1.4 in 1991, the lowest in the NFL that season. It wasn't bad in 1992, climbing all the way to 1.6, equalling the Giants' all-time low for interceptions and again best in the league among passers over 175 attempts. He rushed for 273 yards in 1991, including the highlight reel classic 47-yard rush for a touchdown against the Cardinals. He set the Giants' club record for single season completion percentage at 62.8 on 179 of 285 for 2,032 yards and five touchdowns, and the Giants' single-game completion record of 82.3 with 28 for 34, 368-yard performance against Dallas.

These are just a smattering of his great Giants stats, but let's think Raiders. The *Oakland* Raiders. Yes, the Raiders are "home again" in Oakland, and yes, there are lawyers hulking about with a lawsuit lurking, but never mind. Let Al Davis fuss with that. Let's play ball.

And that's just what the Hoss did on opening day of the 1995 season. He took the raiders up and down the field at the Oakland Coliseum defusing last year's AFC West champions and Super Bowl contenders, the San Diego Chargers, 17-7. This was the intended start for a season in which the Raiders were expected to win the AFC West. His 14-play, 99-yard touchdown drive in the first half showed what Hoss intended to do with the Raiders' revamped offense. It was the right start for a new season that tails on

8

last years' 3,334 yards passing, the second-highest single season total in Raiders history. Hoss completed 263 of 454 passes with 20 touchdowns last year, all career highs. He led the AFC and placed third in the league with a 7.34-yard average per pass. *And*, not one to forget to use his feet when his receivers are all jammed up, he was second on the Raiders in rushing, with 46 carries and two touchdowns.

Do you get the idea the Jeff knows his game and fueled his effort with tons of accountability and guts? He does, but these glory feats are not really what this book is about or why you should read it. It's about *Gruntsville*, that place you have to go through about twice too many times to get to the glory feats. The message here is how to stand tough, stay flexible, useful, eager and ready while surviving the grunt time and rising above it, better for what you learned.

These insights apply to all of us, whatever our job, wherever we see ourselves headed. The only requirement is that you are headed somewhere, somewhere of your own choosing. That choice is the start of accountability, and the lessons the Brothers Hostetler point out on their tour of Gruntsville will speed that progress.

Gruntsville is never pleasant (and circumstances *will* land you there from time-to-time), but if you know your purpose, you will wade through it, and, know what? You will recognize you learned something.

Enjoy.

Jim Tunney, Ed.D., CSP, CPAE
Professional Speaker and Former NFL Referee
Pebble Beach, California
September 4, 1995

GRUNTSVILLE

The world is full of grunts. Miserable little people, wallowing in small, pathetic places, doing insignificant, little things with their lives. This is Gruntsville. And they want out.

It's certainly not a happy place. It's a ghetto filled with bitterly disappointed people, young and old alike. People with dying dreams, broken hearts, and souring dispositions. Their dream of escaping to the big places to be big people doing big things seems next to impossible, so they suffer in silence. Helplessly watching life pass them by. So it seems.

It's no fun being a nobody, doing nothing important, and going nowhere special. And it's not that they planned it this way. You see, most grunts started out their journey in life with high hopes, unbridled optimism and the will to win. The high school athlete dreaming of future stardom. The newlywed bride and groom dreaming of living happily ever after. The young businessman dreaming of building financial empires. The young writer and actor dreaming of Academy Awards. And all the others, dreaming of making important discoveries for, and significant contributions to, their world.

But, unfortunately, it didn't happen. For them, anyway. Their rising balloon of success lost air in the turbulent winds of wail. Unforeseen tragedies derailed their plans, and misfortunate circumstances detoured their route from Starsville to Gruntsville. And once there, they soon lost heart and quit, becoming skeptical, cynical, and increasingly bitter, because life just wasn't working out the way they wanted.

I know. I was there. And so was by brother Jeff.

Oh, we both started out well enough. We were endowed with a fighting, competitive spirit, athleticism, intelligence, optimism, and a will to win.

11

It was enough to get us started toward the never never land of our dreams. And through hard work, dogged determination, and the prayers and faith of our parents, we succeeded, until the storms of tragedy and failure blew us off course, washing us ashore the beaches of Gruntsville.

But it was there, in this miserable, unhappy place, that we uncovered some of life's greatest secrets, and treasures-- the fields of diamonds, and nuggets of gold, that could be mined from life's miserable mishaps, and devastating disasters.

We didn't know it at the time. But although there was no joy in Gruntsville for us, there were valuable lessons to be learned. Lessons that eventually transformed us from grunts to rising stars. Lessons that changed us into the people we were created to be, doing the things we were created to do.

What about you?

Have the storms of tragedy derailed your plans? Have miserable mishaps and unforeseen circumstances blown you off course? Have the tides of trouble washed away your dream castles in the sands of time. And have you found yourself inside the gates of Gruntsville?

If so, you're not alone.

There are hundreds and thousands of others who have been exiled here.

Grunts who have been betrayed by life. Dealt a bad hand. Been treated unfairly. Overlooked. Not given a chance to show what they could do.

They feel insignificant. Unimportant. Of no value to anyone. Given only grunt work to perform without the opportunity for greater challenges.

Life for them has become tiring. Boring. And depressing. Simply the pits. And they have lost confidence in themselves and their world, with no hope for a better tomorrow. Secretly wanting to just quit and give up on everyone and everything.

If you feel this way, then this message is for you. From the boardroom to the locker room to the classroom to the family room, if you're tired of feeling like a grunt and a nobody, performing meaningless, insignificant tasks, and unable to shake off its depressing affects, then read on.

We want you to learn what we did. Some of life's simple, little lessons that will transform you from a grunt to a rising star. Lessons on mastery, learning, perspective, accountability, drudgery, reconciliation, time management, structure, prayer, hope, faith, failure, love, and climbing the stairway to success. These are some of the lessons I was taught while a grunt--a practice dummy, on Penn State's maroon platoon. And they're also some of the lessons my brother Jeff was taught while a grunt--a third-string quarterback, with the New York Giants. We're confident you too can learn, and benefit from these lessons just like we did.

In fact, we'll take you step by step into and through Gruntsville's "Due Time Dimension"-- the secret place of struggle, where wings of faith are developed, and perspective is cultivated. Where tempestuous transitions give way to tempered transformations. Where the human heart, mind, and spirit is repaired, renewed, and restored. And where purpose, meaning and fulfillment are conceived.

Our goal is to help you recognize and cultivate the inner qualities, attitudes, skills and values that lead to success. Attitudes and values birthed from timeless truths, not transient realities.

So whether you're a grunt on the gridiron, in the classroom, at home or at work, don't lose heart. And please, don't quit in your quest for life's best. There's good news ahead for you as you take the time to study and apply the lessons we have in store for you. There's much to learn. There's a promise to possess. And it all awaits you in the contact sport of Gruntsville.

Third and goal.

Sprinting out to my right, football firmly in hand, I looked for an opening. Any opening. But what I encountered was a brutal Chicago Bears defense closing in on me.

It was a spine chilling moment. Mike Singletary, the notorious all pro linebacker and headhunter, had set his deadly, lazer like, beady little infrared sights on me from his inside position, while 350 pound tackle William Perry, the "refrigerator", threatened to steam roll me from the outside.

What were my options? Pass. Keep the ball and run. Or play dead.

I decided to tuck the football under my arm and run.

With one eye on the goal line, and the other on the rear ends of my New York Giants offensive linemen, I frantically scrambled along the line of scrimmage searching for the smallest opening to duck into. One that Singletary or Perry couldn't fit in to.

Spotting a hairline crack between two of my blockers, not a butt crack mind you, I lunged forward in a desperate attempt to cross the goal line while avoiding the onslaught of my attackers.

When I opened my eyes, I still had the football clutched under my arm. I was still breathing. And better yet, I had scored six points for my team. Putting us ahead for keeps, and getting us into the National Football League Conference Championship.

I'll always remember that keeper. Because it reminds me of when I was a kid. My days back home on the farm, in the back yard, playing football with my brothers.

You see, Doug and Ron are five and six years older than me, and at that time appeared just as big and mean as Singletary and Perry. Back then I only reached as tall as their

14

arm pits, while Todd, my younger brother by a year, stood a little shorter. But that didn't stop us from playing football against them. In fact, we loved it. And even though they would often play on their knees to make things fair, they never seemed to stay there, particularly if we happened to break open down the sideline on a long run.

They enjoyed hammering us with forearms and body blocks. And I guess we liked it too. We kept going back for more even though they would occasionally slam us into the electric cow-puncher fence that separated the yard from the cow pasture. Perhaps that's why we run so fast today.

Yep, football in the backyard with the Hoss brothers on Sunday afternoon. Sandwiched between church and chores, it was the place where Sunday School lessons of love, humility, and mercy slammed hard against personal pride, power, and conquest. Where Mennonite beliefs of pacifism, restraint, and peace, did battle with aggression, conflict, and hate.

In Ecclesiastical terms it was a season for everything under the sun. A season of laughing and crying. Tearing and mending. Trash talking and silence. Dancing and mourning.

And it continued. Sunday after Sunday. Round after round. Toe to toe. Until old man winter sounded the final bell.

Driven by an insatiable appetite for competition, and a will to win, Todd and I would challenge our older brothers in a backyard game of football, season after season. Younger against older. Smaller against bigger. Just for the chance, the opportunity, to beat them.

Now I can't recall if we ever did beat them, or even come close, and maybe that tells you something about all the hits I took to the head since then, but as shocking as those times were, it was great preparation for the body slams and relentless poundings Gruntsville was going to deliver on us in the coming years. Not to mention the crushing hits I was to take from Leon Seals and Bruce Smith in Super Bowl XXV.

Now I can't remember when Todd and I started closing the gap between Ron and Doug, when size and strength started evenening out the playing field. But I can recall a moment in the backyard between Ron and me, when things seemed to change for good between us. He remembers too. So I'm going to let him tell his version of what happened.

Well, I remember the day and the play that Jeff finally got so ticked off at me for slamming and throwing him around, that he faked a hand-off to Todd, kept the ball for himself, and ran straight at me. I waited for him to fake and cut away from me like he always did, but it never happened. With fire in his belly, and revenge in his eyes, he threw himself, kamikaze style, hard into my gut, almost knocking me off my feet. Surprised, and a little shaken, I countered with a forearm to his chest, and watched him crash to the ground as he recoiled in pain.

But he never said a word. He just looked up at me with a look in his eye I had never seen before. And when he stood up, I noticed for the first time how much bigger he had gotten. He wasn't my little brother anymore. He was almost my height, his legs were thicker and stronger, and his shoulders had broadened. So had his head and heart, both now seemed a lot more determined and stubborn because he repeated the whole thing again. He ran right smack into me, hoping to catch me off guard and knock me on my butt, but I recovered fast enough to knock him down once more. And this time it was a little harder than the last.

And when he stood up, he gave me that look again. A silent stare that seemed to say, "you may have knocked me down again, but in my heart I'm still standing."

Thinking I finally knocked some sense into him, I waited for his next play, expecting him to try something different. But he didn't. He did it again!

This time, after charging into me like a raging bull, I

16

delivered a forearm into his chest with everything I had, expecting to flip him backwards, head over heels. But it didn't happen. He dropped the ball, grabbed hold of me, and tried to wrestle me to the ground. It turned into a little brawl. And we exchanged some words. But when things finally settled down, his eyes told me all I had to know. From now on, things were going to be different. He wasn't going to be pushed around anymore. He was going to do some punishing of his own.

A year later, the same thing happened with Todd. There came a time and place I had to recognize that he too had closed the gap between us. And over the years we all developed a great respect for each other because we used those moments to sharpen one another as iron sharpens iron.

Now, looking back, those times remind us that life is indeed a contact sport. That there's going to be days when life body slams you with shocking hits. Times when it will stiff arm you with trouble. Moments when it will trip you up, kick you, poke you in the eye, call you names, and almost knock you out. There will be times it will shatter your teeth, ring your bell, take advantage of your weaknesses, test your endurance, play games with your mind, and tempt you to quit. But eventually, if you hang in there, apply yourself, and determine to get bigger, stronger and better, you'll eventually close the gap between you and your problems.

I thank God for those times. They helped me appreciate my brothers more. My family more. The game of football. And the lessons that could be learned from life's continuous, crushing contacts.

So as you grope through Gruntsville, don't let the knockdowns and forearms of your struggle quench your competitive spirit or bench your passion for excellence. Do as I did, look at them as though they were your big brothers, there to challenge and help you grow. To sharpen you as iron sharpens iron. And just as surely as the seasons of life change for the good, so will you, if you apply the lessons of Gruntsville.

So buckle your chin strap, call your next play, take the snap, and run towards your goal. Along the way expect to encounter the Singletary's and Perry's of the world. Expect to get knocked down, tramped on, and pushed around. But remember this, if you don't keep getting up and running at it again, you will never bridge the gap, or know what could have been.

MISSING THE POINT OF GRUNTSVILLE

In four seconds, the biggest game of my life would be over. Just one point and a 47-yard fieldgoal attempt separated our New York Giants and the Buffalo Bills from the world championship. As the Bills' kicker lined up the fieldgoal that would determine the winner of Super Bowl XXV, I knew the result was out of my control. But I felt a deep sense of fulfillment and peace as I waited for the kick that would be seen and heard around the world.

My journey to get here had been long and difficult. In fact, if you would have asked me a couple of weeks ago if it were possible for me to be the starting quarterback in Super Bowl XXV, I would've said no. Why? Because things never seemed to work out for me. Somehow, some way, I never seemed to catch a break, or get a shot at really showing what I could do.

As a matter of fact, it hadn't been too long ago that my entire career seemed out of my control. I remember coming home to my wife Vicky and saying, "I told them I want to be traded, Vick."

She glanced up at me with understanding eyes.

It wasn't the first time she had heard those words. She had watched me gulp down my pride time and time again in season after frustrating season as a backup quarterback with the Giants. As the daughter of my West Virginia University coach, Don Nehlen, Vicky understood what the cloud of second-guessers and critics could do to a man's self-assurance.

"Jeff, you're too good to be standing around on the sidelines," she'd reassure me. "I'll move anywhere if it means you'll get your shot at playing."

I have never accepted the role of backup quarterback. When relegated to the sidelines at Penn State, I had transferred to West Virginia. Given the chance to prove myself there, I had helped the Mountaineers break through the nation's top 20 ranking and earn trips to several bowl games. As a result, the Giants had chosen me in the prime third round of the NFL draft. By all appearances, I was earmarked as the Giants' quarterback of the future.

But after my first few pro seasons, it appeared that I was the quarterback with no future. And I felt utterly powerless to do anything about it. As a backup quarterback, I wasn't even allowed to take a practice snap with the first team offense.

By the end of my third year, I had reached a point of desperation. I had asked to be on special teams, play wide receiver, anything--just to get into the game.

I knew that the longer I was denied the chance to prove myself, the more the coaches, sportswriters, and fans would doubt that I could play in the NFL. And to be honest, there were times when even I doubted what I could do anymore.

During the games, I paced the sidelines, toting my little clipboard as if I were playing a board game. Aided by hours of studying and a photographic memory, I could often predict what was going to happen just by watching the opposing team's defensive lineup. But what good did that do from the sidelines? I couldn't challenge the opposing team's backup quarterback to a clipboard duel.

In 1988, I had been granted a rare chance to play against the New Orleans Saints when our starting quarterback, Phil Simms, had gotten hurt. My chance at last, I thought. After all these years of enduring sideline duty and skeptics, I can finally let my performance on the field answer all doubts.

At first, the coaches tied my hands with running play after running play. Then, suddenly, I spotted Stephen Baker down field and connected for an 85-yard touchdown pass play. Before the half ended, I had begun to click with the offense and we were moving the ball.

I figured I was on my way to a healthy first start. But as I walked through the tunnel out toward the playing field for the second half, an assistant coach pulled me up short. Coach Parcells was yanking me out to put in the third string quarterback.

That was all I needed to hear. After the game, I strode into the locker room and demanded, "Get me out of here."

The pot that had been simmering so long inside me just exploded. I meted out my feelings to the press, my agent, players--anyone who cared to listen. I wanted to be traded immediately.

My agent, Rob Bennett, suggested I sleep on the idea. He found me just as determined when he called the next morning. I was sick and tired of having my career hang on what the coach explained as "a gut feeling."

To my dismay, Giants owner George Young mixed the trade.

That night, I walked into my son's room and leaned over him as he slept. He lay there so peacefully--so far removed from the stormy trials of my life in the NFL. Of course he had no idea how angry I was. Or how hopeless, frustrated, and stuck I felt. How I secretly wished life would be easy for once. Just go the way I wanted it. Just once.

It seemed that whatever plan God might have had for my life somehow had gotten lost in the translation. Where was God in disasters, betrayals, and now, in the tribulations of my life?

And then it struck me.

Just then I remembered the terrible trial my son went through as he pushed his way into this world. How close we came to losing him. And how he fought and struggled to gain every minute of life he could.

The doctor had delivered the prognosis to Vicky and me with the impact of a sledgehammer. Jason had a host of life-jeopardizing cardiopulmonary problems. He was cyanotic--he had turned blue from not getting enough oxygen into his bloodstream.

Before we even had a chance to hold him, he was whisked away to intensive care. Our first baby, the little boy we had waited so long to hold, lay in an incubator, IV's sticking out of his little arms and looking a deathly blue. I remember touching his arm gently and whispering, "It's going to be okay, little guy. You just hang in there."

But I felt so helpless at the time. Unable to believe those words myself. The wonderful future Vick and I had planned for Jason had come crashing down. All in a moment.

But even though he couldn't speak a word at that time, his fighting, indomitable spirit spoke volumes. Each breath, each heartbeat penned another line of tenacious courage and perseverance in the pages of his short, new life. In his own little wordless way, he seemed to be saying, "I believe you dad, I'm going to make it."

Four traumatic heart operations later, Jason appears to be out of the woods. An outstanding surgeon at our hometown West Virginia University Medical Center had surgically corrected Jason's defective pulmonary valve. And yet, the doctors reminded us, we could never be sure. It was just something we'd have to live with, just like Jason would always live with the long scars down the middle of his chest.

And now tonight, my slumbering son was silently reminding me of my words and his perseverance. If he hung in there, then so should I.

And so I did.

As I walked out of my son's room that night, I was determined to fight the odds, and struggle through the circumstances regardless of the outcome. And it was reassuring to know that no matter what happened on the playing field, I was loved by a wife and family that didn't care if I were the starting quarterback or the groundskeeper.

They loved me for who I was, not for what I did.

As I look back on that night I thank God for it. I can look back and see God's hand of providence guiding me. But at the time, I just saw another obstacle hindering me from reaching God's elusive plan for my life. I learned a very important lesson and gained a very significant perspective on things. That life is very precious and fragile. That at any moment it can be snatched away. That we are to live determined, purposeful, and meaningful lives while we can. And not spend our days foolishly worrying over trivial matters or pursuing frivolous, meaningless things.

That experience also made me think about my extended family--Mom and Dad and my six brothers and sisters. I had called them often to vent my frustrations. I always found a sympathetic ear, but they always ended up with the same message: "Your time's coming, it's coming. Hang in there."

Dad had lived out those words. His example of perseverance had shown us that just because things get rough, you never quit. You simply don't put that word into your vocabulary.

I remember that hot summer night when Mom raced through the house waking us out of deep sleep. "Kids--wake up--the barn's burning! The barn's burning!" I awoke to the yellow glow of the blaze and the cracking sound of burning timbers. Even at the age of six, I knew something dreadful was happening.

As we children huddled together in horror, we watched our barn burn to the ground. Not only did we lose the newly-stacked crop of hay, but our precious livestock as well. Dad and Ron had jumped in to save our favorite dog, Duke, just before timbers crashed down.

Just weeks before, Dad had been laid up with what the doctors suspected was a brain tumor. Our fellow Mennonite neighbors had pitched in to harvest our hay and stack it all into the barn. Now, our neighbor's expression of love and our family's livelihood lay in a smoldering heap of ash.

I remember Dad's dejected face as he helplessly watched our livelihood go up in smoke. We knew Dad felt the pain and frustration, but he never said anything. He just got back on his feet and set about the task of rebuilding his farm. Somehow, some way, Dad managed to climb out of the ashes and set his face toward rebuilding our future.

Dad never gave up. Not even a few years later, when the new roof on our long chicken house suddenly collapsed under the weight of a heavy snow. Dad was a living example of perseverance. He competed daily as a farmer--against nature and adversity. Hard winters, continual equipment breakdowns, and unstable prices continually tested his will and determination. Dad knew the meaning of hard work, and he knew how to handle hardship.

My brother Ron remembers: "The Mennonite work ethic is simple: you don't quit. The farm is a great lesson in problem solving, of getting up a lot when you're down. You have to believe that somehow God's going to get you through it."

"We learned from Dad's example. He just kept getting up every morning and going back out there."

I agree. We learned just by watching Dad work and continue to work even when things would break down or didn't go well. He would just continue plugging away. I realized that things weren't always going to go the way you want them to, but you just keep plugging away until you accomplish what you set out to do."

Mom was the same way. Everything she did, she did wholeheartedly. Her spirit about life was just tenacious. She went after things. And If there was one thing she was going to do, it was to raise her kids with the belief that God was capable of doing the impossible in our lives if we just didn't quit.

Well, over the years, I got to the point where I finally believed the Lord had a plan for me that in due time and in due course, was going to unfold. I was determined to be ready. Both Dad and my father-in-law hammered away at the same theme: be patient, do your part to be prepared, be ready to go at a moment's notice.

During a typically cold and cloudy December day in Giants' stadium, I breathed warm air into my hands on the sidelines. But on this particular day, something unexpected happened, leading to an incredible chain of events that would soon turn my world upside down.

I had for six and a half years applied myself to mastering our offensive plays, analyzing opponents' defenses and trying to make a contribution to the team in any way I could.

And today, it happened. My moment came. Simms went down with an ankle injury and I went in. After six and one-half long seasons of struggle, I finally, had an opportunity to escape my sideline prison and prove my critics wrong.

Ironically, we were playing the Buffalo Bills--the same team I'd later face in the Super Bowl. This time, the Bills outscored us. While disappointed, I still felt elated that I'd finally be guiding the team the next week. I imagined all week in my mind the plays we'd put together against the Phoenix Cardinals.

Dream turned to reality when I hit Rodney Hampton for an electrifying 78-yard touchdown play. I ran the ball nine times--five more than our running back, Otis Anderson. I completed five or eight passes on first downs alone. It felt incredibly good to fall into the rhythm of moving the team up and down the field.

When the clock finally ran out, I was holding the ball and a satisfying 20-19 victory. At last, I dared to believe, I was on my way to success in the National Football League. I couldn't wait for the upcoming playoffs.

As it turned out, though, my family and I seemed to be the only ones who entertained notions of success. Even our hometown New York media doomed me to failure. The New York Times tactfully summed up my first four years in the NFL: "no pass attempts, no completions, no yards, no percentage, no touchdowns and no interceptions."

Even our own head coach appeared at a loss for optimism, warning the press, "It isn't going to be perfect."

Beneath the media hype, I knew the playoffs were won or lost through action, not words. I brought to the task years of hard work, a determination born of trial, and a growing belief that God did, indeed, have a plan He was fulfilling for my life.

We surprised every last one of the doomsayers with an astounding 31-3 playoff victory over the Chicago Bears. We now set our sights on the seemingly invincible San Francisco 49'ers, let by legendary quarterback Joe Montana. Predictably, the media doomsayer articles reappeared, contrasting the Super Bowl-winning Montana with the inexperienced Hostetler.

I decided to let the scoreboard write the story.

It was a classic, "knock-down, drag-em-out" football game. And when it was all over, a nationwide television audience witnessed what all had said couldn't be done. Our last-minute drive set up a heart-stopping Matt Bahr fieldgoal to win the game and a trip to "The Show", Super Bowl XXV.

As I waited in my hotel room before this game, which would be seen by millions around the world, I felt a remarkable sense of peace and confidence. I knew I could do it. Because I had prepared myself well, I had no doubts about my ability to do the job. I just wanted to take advantage of the situation at hand.

During the first half of the Super Bowl, a couple of fierce shots almost knocked me right out of the game. On a passing play, 270-pound end Leon Seals nearly leveled the life out of me. Even after inhaling smelling salts on the sidelines, I could hardly see straight. On the next series, All-Pro end Bruce Smith corralled me in the end zone for a two-point safety. Thankfully, I held onto the ball and prevented a Bills' touchdown, which would have given them the margin of victory.

Six minutes into the third quarter, we were trailing 12-10. I was looking at third down and 13 long yards between a first down and an unyielding Bills defense. I bent into the huddle and glanced around at the sweating, determined faces of ten men who had come to win.

"Half-right-62-comeback-dig."

As I leaned over the center, I surveyed the Bills' defensive alignment. Recognizing it immediately, I knew our play would work.

I took the snap, pedaled back to pass, and spotted my man eight yards up field. I drilled the ball to wideout Mark Ingram, who took it and weaved, spun and dived his way past lunging defenders and the first down marker. A few plays later, I stuffed the ball into the gut of Otis Anderson, who stormed into the end zone with the go-ahead touchdown, 17-12. I knew we were within reach of one of the greatest Super Bowl victories of all time.

After a fourth-quarter TD by the Bills, Matt Bahr's clutch fieldgoal provided us with the one-point margin that stood on the scoreboard with four seconds remaining.

As the Bills kicker eyed his target, I knelt down on one knee and took it all in. I felt really, really good. I didn't know what the kicker was going to do--miss it or make it. I just resigned myself to the fact that I had given it all I could, and there wasn't anything else I could do at this point.

I watched that decisive kick sail up high and deep toward the goalposts until it finally dropped to the ground--wide to the right of its target. The fans in the stands and millions of TV viewers around the world exploded in pandemonium.

But I was alone with my thoughts. It was done.

My stormy trial was over. I was vindicated.

"They said you couldn't do it, Hoss. They said you couldn't do it", yelled a teammate of mine in the locker room, referring to the cloud of critics and reporters who had doubted my ability to lead our team to the title of "World Champions."

I wasn't about to rub it in. I only knew that somehow God had arranged the opportunity. And that He had enabled me to do the best I could, where I was at, with what I had.

I had fulfilled a goal that seemed impossible only weeks before. And I knew that it only incidentally had to do with that pigskin bouncing on the turf.

It had more to do with learning the lessons of Gruntsville. Lessons that developed my character, and strengthened my inner self.

It had more to do with growing stronger through seasons of struggle, mastering the mystery of the Due Time Dimension and developing wing muscles of faith.

It had more to do with recognizing and cultivating the inner qualities and attitudes that bring fulfillment and meaning to life. Attitudes, skills, and values that go beyond modern man's view of success.

Well, that was several years ago. Today, I'm the quarterback of the Oakland Raiders. I became a free agent, left the New York Giants, and started a new season with a team that possesses great talent and a tenacious appetite for excellence.

We too, have set our sights on the title of "World Champions." And personally, I'm going to do everything I can to help get us there. But as I prepare for our next season I'm concerned about the "images of success" that are being transmitted by the media. The crisis of character that exists in our homes, our communities, and our world. The "in your face" attitude that is permeating our culture. The "me first",

"I want it now", and "I've got mine" values that are crippling the capacity, and capabilities of future generations.

I'm concerned that it's creating a generation of people believing the message that says dominance and conquest at any price is the ultimate goal in life. That the pursuit of money, power, pleasure, and leisure activities are the only significant sources of happiness.

It seems people are preoccupied with appearances and immediate sensual gratification. They identify winning with looking young and beautiful, or having fame and fortune. Speaking from my own personal experience, this kind of identification to winning is deceiving and destructive. And it will ultimately lead to a generation of people pursuing and achieving goals that will not bring total fulfillment, meaning, or lasting satisfaction to their lives.

Now I 'm passionate about the pursuit of excellence. I'm a competitor, and I'm fervent in my belief in being a winner and seeking success. But I want to tell you something. What you see on television is not all that it's cracked up to be. It has a way of making people and things appear bigger, better and more important than they really are. It has a way of making you feel like a nobody if you aren't rich or famous.

Now you can do what you want. But please, don't miss the point I'm trying to make. Don't kick your life wide right by pursuing the wrong goals or taking the easy way out when you get stuck in Gruntsville. You will only end up on the short end of the score and the losing side of the field if you do.

When life smacks you in the face with failure, disappointment, heartache, suffering, and difficult circumstances, and be sure that it will, you will have a decision to make. To either quit, make excuses, escape into drugs, sex and pleasure, become fatalistic and depressed, settle for less than you could be, or work your way through it. Unfortunately, I've seen too many people choose the former. And I don't want their fatal choice to become yours.

You see, Gruntsville is inevitable for all of us. It's no respecter of persons. Everyone will eventually come to this place in their lives, imaginary or not, where they will have to make a very important decision. To either struggle, grope, and perhaps painfully persevere in order to grow, or else quit. The choice is yours. In other words, Gruntsville is a place that leads to either renewal or ruin. And you must decide right now, that as you journey through it, you're not going to let it ruin you.

So please, don't miss my point. As you eye up your target--your dreams and goals in life and focus on what you need to do to accomplish them, don't lose heart and quit when the pressure is applied. I'm here to tell you good things can and will happen for you if you don't. Just follow through on the instructional lessons, gridiron explanations, and down home on the farm illustrations we're going to share with you in the following pages, and you'll soon be kicking game winners through the uprights as you discover the secret to this mysterious place called Gruntsville. See you at the end of the game.

"Aw nuts, Hostetler! Nuts! Get on the ball! Get on the ball!", screamed a venomous, Joe Paterno. His poisonous verbal strike hit me with the speed and accuracy of a rattlesnake.

The football I was supposed to have in my grasp wasn't there. It was flopping around on the grassy turf like a fish out of water.

The center had short-snapped it off my hands, causing a fumble. But I never had the opportunity to explain that to Joe.

In the blink of an eye, coach Paterno had accused, tried, and judged me guilty of fumbling the football. And the only recourse I had at the moment was to carry out his sentence.

Scared and humiliated, I scrambled after that pigskin like a raving lunatic. Finally hooking it with a right paw, as I sucked for air, and the courage to look up while I laid motionless at the feet of Paterno.

Peeking out of the corner of my helmet, I could see the smirks and smiles of my teammates. But Paterno's face told me all I had to know. It had a pathetic look of disgust written all over it. You might of thought I had just lost the national championship for him or something.

In that moment, I felt betrayed by the coach who only months before had recruited me to Penn State with compelling words and flattering compliments.
A coach who promised to give me a shot at success, not shoot me down before I could begin. One who had convinced me I had the right stuff to succeed in big time college football.

For most of my scholastic career I had been a successful Pennsylvania quarterback. Enough to earn All-State honors and a position on Pennsylvania's elite Big Thirty-Three All Star football team with the likes of N.F.L. Hall of Famer, Tony Dorsett.

I had been recruited by the nations best Division I colleges, and had the grades to attend the Ivy League school of my choice. Penn State however, was relatively close to our dairy and poultry farm in southwest Pennsylvania and it had a big-time program and a big-time coach who was different, in many respects, to all the others.

Yes, Paterno was different all right. I remember being disappointed the first time I saw him on television. He didn't look like the legend I had read about. He had a strange accent and wore a pair of big, black, eye-glasses that resembled the bottom of coke bottles. He looked like the second coming of Steve Erkel. He just didn't fit my image of a successful head football coach.

But watching him win over the years, and listening to his philosophy of coaching during a recruiting trip to our house, eventually won over over my faith and trust in his program. That is, until now.

Now, he appeared ruthless and intolerant, like a Dr. Jekyl and Mr. Hyde, as he went off on me in a spitting, ranting rage. Looking as though he enjoyed plundering what little self-respect and confidence I had left.

It was obvious this was the dark side of that once friendly, trustworthy coach who had greeted me at the doorstep of our farmhouse a few months ago. Now I was only a freshman quarterback. Inexperienced and prone to making mistakes. And it was only my first practice. But that fumbled snap was my entry into Gruntsville. And Paterno was the welcoming committee.

No sooner had I stood up, when in front of everybody, he began lecturing me on the importance and necessity of jumping on a loose football, regardless of who was at fault. That I had the responsibility to pursue, protect, possess, and preserve the football for the sake of our team. No excuses. No explanations. Just get it done. His way.

Well, as I walked off the field that day from practice, I

wanted to forget every miserable thing about it. Put it out of my memory forever. But I couldn't.

Yeah, I knew Paterno was just trying to make a point. And he was trying to make it stick. But the way he went about it left me with a sick feeling in my stomach. A feeling that things would get worse. And you know what? Things did.

When the season ended, Joe made a decision to switch me to defense. From quarterback to linebacker. Now I had also played linebacker in high school, but needless to say I was almost devastated with the change. It meant the death of my dream to become Penn State's next All-American quarterback. A dream that had inspired me. A dream that had kept me working, sweating and struggling to fulfill. Now it was gone. And I had to start all over again.

Well, that was the day I bellied up on the beaches of Gruntsville. The day my life went from bad to worse. The day I lost trust in the words of the man who had recruited me to such a God-forsakened wasteland. The day my relationship with Joe went from friend to foe in his house of woe.

"Keep hustling, something good will happen", spouted coach Paterno. "Sure, that's easy for you to say", I would mumble under my breath, as I sat with my head down, listening to him preach to me and my teammates in our Penn State locker room. I was sick and tired of his sermons. They were a broken record. I just couldn't believe him anymore, even though he was one of the most successful college football coaches of all time.

Why couldn't I believe him anymore? Why had I lost trust in him and his words? Because they weren't true. At least for me, anyway. No matter how hard I seemed to try to make something good happen, nothing ever did. Everything seemed to be going wrong, and I was stuck on a squad of practice dummies wearing maroon jerseys, called the maroon platoon.

You see, for me, the maroon platoon was a place for misfit athletes. An insignificant place for orphaned athletes struggling to break out of a cocoon of failure. In other words, it was Paterno's dog house. His house of woe. A small place, for little people like me, to perform meaningless grunt work for everyone else.

Everyone in our insignificant little village of Gruntsville wore a maroon jersey. They were the ugliest, sorriest looking jerseys you could imagine. They were tattered and torn, patched and re-patched, never thrown away, just used and reused by a sorry looking, rag-tag bunch of so called "losers". Run of the mill players who were quickly written off by their coaches as average.

In reality, our maroon jerseys symbolized frustration and failure. It was the "Scarlet Letter" of jerseys, and it reminded us of our marooned existence. We were left alone as though we were lepers. Slowly losing touch with the world. Slowly wasting away in our time capsule of decline and despair.

Now I was one of the lesser known, the least known, and the unknowns. And nobody seemed to notice me. Nobody seemed to care. Sometimes the coaches didn't even know my name. And I hated being used as a practice dummy for the known, the better known and the famous.

To me, Gruntsville was a dead end street for dead end athletes. A place for dejected, neglected and rejected castaways. A miserable, wretched, deplorable place for a platoon of marooned misfits. Stuck in a cocoon of grief, regret and despair.

Now all of this nonsense was enough to make me feel like quitting. Particularly after giving all I could, day after day, practice after stink'n practice, for the better part of two seasons. Nobody, I thought. Nobody deserved this kind of treatment. It was all so unfair. And I pointed my finger of blame at everyone, and everything, but me.

You probably know what I mean. You know what I'm talking about, when you haven't been given a chance to prove yourself. When bad things happen to you through no fault of your own. When circumstances and tough luck prevent you from reaching your goal and fulfilling your dream. And especially, when someone with the power to change your destiny, becomes your worst nightmare.

Who is your worst nightmare? Who is the one that seems to have control over the circumstances of your life? The one who holds the key to unlocking the door of opportunity for you? Your worst nightmare could be any of a number of different people or things. It could even be a habit, compulsion, or behavior that controls you and limits your potential.

Well, one thing is sure. Gruntsville is no picnic. The nightmare is real. Mine certainly was. Every practice reminded me of my misery in Joe's house of woe, and there seemed to be no escape, except one. Quitting.

I was tired.

I was tired of Paterno. Tired of his lectures. Tired of practice. Tired of the same old routine. Tired of doing all the "little things" I was supposed to do. Tired of nothing going right. Tired of the drudgery and difficulty associated with football. Tired of Gruntsville.

Life as a grunt had taken its toll. I wanted out of this miserable place. Off the island of our marooned misfit platoon. And the sooner, the better.

So after our Friday's practice I returned to my apartment with the intent of not going back. I had had enough. I had lost heart. And I had come home to quit.

So as I collapsed on the sofa, I let out a desperate sigh of resignation. Sort of like a distress signal as I felt my ship of dreams slowly sink into its watery grave.

But on my way down, something unexpected happened. I don't know why or how, but out of the quiet darkness came a response to my S.O.S. It was a simple response. And it was this.

D-o-n-'t l-o-s-e h-e-a-r-t i-n d-o-i-n-g g-o-o-d, f-o-r i-n d-u-e t-i-m-e y-o-u w-i-l-l r-e-a-p i-f y-o-u d-o-n-'t q-u-i-t!

"Now where did that come from?", I asked myself. And then I remembered. It was a message I planted in my memory banks long ago. A truth I had sown as a child. And now, after all those years of lying dormant in fallow ground, it had germinated.

It's kind of hard to explain, but in my darkest moment, that simple little message sprouted an attitude of hope in the dark soil of sorrow I was buried in. And like a plow, my mind kept turning it over and over until it worked its way up to the surface of my will. I decided not to quit.

As I walked out the door of my apartment the next

morning, I was determined to break new ground, to see my way up and through my soiled circumstances regardless of the outcome. I was ready to go the distance whatever the cost, even after discovering we were to scrimmage the first team offense that morning. So I prepared myself to pay the ultimate price, to make one last supreme sacrifice for the good of "Old State."

Well, midway into the first quarter, and after a series of hard hitting running plays by their offense that bruised and battered our maroon platoon halfway down the field, they ran a sweep--right at me. Their entire offensive line came charging at me like a herd of buffalo. They were snorting and snarling. The dust was flying. The ground was shaking. And I was the only one standing in their path of destruction.

I quickly glanced around for help. Nobody home.

My survival instinct kicked in. You know, the fight or flight response? Self preservation told me to get out of there. An inner winning will told me to stand my ground. This was insane.

But then it happened. Again. Just when it looked like this rushing, pounding wave of brutality would crush me with its deadly force, my mind flashed back to a picture perfect tackle I saw Jack Ham of the Pittsburgh Steelers make the week before. He performed like a bull fighter, dodging and sidestepping the opposing linemen until he got to the ball carrier to make the tackle.

Now I wasn't about to pretend I was Jack Ham, but it was worth a shot. So I took it. I side-stepped the first big o'l boy that came at me. Not bad. I juked out the next big lunkhead with a head and shoulder fake. Things were getting better. But when I looked up, I was staring into the fiery red eyes of an over-sized rhino named Tom Rafferty. Raff was the team captain, he later became an All-American and then All-Pro with the Dallas Cowboys. He was foaming at the mouth, his nostrils were flared, his biceps pulsated with power, and his vehometh growl beckoned for blood.

My last ditch effort to get out of his way failed in technique, yet partly worked. All the muscle fibers in my body screamed for mercy as I took his hit in my mid section. The force of his impact knocked me back on my heels in an upright position so I instinctively grabbed hold of the back of his shoulder pads and hung on while the momentum spun us around. It was a bronco ride I'll never forget.

After going full circle with him, I unlocked my death grip and watched an amazing thing happen. Raff went rolling off into the dirt, headfirst while I was left standing. In fact, the momentum had spun me around into the path of the ball carrier who had been cruising undetected behind Raff like a stealth fighter-jet. And he had the look of shock on his face when he saw me set the cross-hairs of my helmet on his gut. So with lightning quick speed, and enough impact to force the air out of his lungs, I exploded into him like a smart bomb, vaporizing him five yards behind the line of scrimmage.

No sooner did I get back on my feet after making the tackle, when I was mobbed by my maroon platoon teammates. And I couldn't help but wonder where they all came from all of a sudden.

But to top it off, as I walked back to the huddle, I heard that all too familiar high pitched voice say to me, "Good job, Hostetler." It was Paterno. He had seen everything. But this time his tone, and his look was much different from that first day of practice I had two years ago.

Now I can't remember much more that happened that day. But I do remember walking off that field with a hopeful heart, and stout spirit. I was proud to be a grunt. Especially one that just schooled our All-American captain. And proud to be on the maroon platoon. But I was more proud that I didn't quit. Otherwise I would have missed all of this. Better yet, I would've missed what was to come.

FROM SOW TO GROW

I walked into the locker room next morning to discover a dark, navy blue jersey hanging in my locker. Only the first team defense wore this colored jersey.

Thinking it was a mistake, or that the equipment manager was pulling a prank, I handed it back in to him. But when I did, he just smiled and told me to see coach Paterno.

What? I was puzzled. Even a little troubled, trying to recall if I had done anything wrong. I didn't know what to think. So with jersey in hand, I went into Joe's dressing room with fear and trembling.

I'll never forget that moment as I entered the room and he looked up at me behind those dark, heavy shaded glasses of his. He glanced over to my linebacker coach, then turned to me and asked if I wanted to start in our season opening game against Temple University on Saturday.

He said he had noticed some changes in my performance lately. Good changes. Changes that convinced him I was ready to play. And that I could make a valuable contribution to our team. I couldn't believe what I was hearing.

I walked back out into the locker room in a daze. Some of my teammates thought I had been cut from the squad when they saw my face. But when I pulled that dark, navy jersey down over my shoulder pads, they realized, along with me, that I had just emerged from my maroon cocoon. It was done. I was on my way out of Gruntsville.

Paterno was right. Keep hustling and something good will happen. Take care of the little things and the big things will take care of themselves. In that moment my coke bottled nightmare had reappeared as a genie in a bottle. All along Paterno had been there, working my wish. Teaching, training, trying and testing to forge and temper in me the kind of inner steel I needed to succeed. And the great thing about it all is, if it could happen for me, it could happen for anyone.

But how did this all come about and why? What happened to me inside the woeful walls of my maroon cocoon anyway? And did it have anything to do with the outcome experienced by my brother Jeff?

Well, it was all a mystery to me at first. Sort of like a combination lock that had me guessing, trying, and spinning my way through a combination of attitudes, skills and values, learning components if you will, until I discovered the genetic code that unlocked the door to opportunity and success.

In reality, what I actually discovered was the secret to the Due Time Dimension. And although I didn't recognize its structure, range, scope, magnitude, or purpose at first, it ultimately became the cornerstone of my life plan. The core curriculum of my learning experience inside the wailing walls of Gruntsville. And not just for me, but for my brother Jeff too.

You see, we discovered something very unusual about the Due Time Dimension. That over time, it secreted a kind of mental, emotional, and spiritual growth hormone for success as we struggled to grow. That it produced a kind of progressive, incremental, and continuous living stimulant that stirred up in us and set in motion a planned process of growth and differentiation so we could reach our goals and maximize our potential. And the interesting thing we discovered about its secretion action was this, the more we struggled, the more we grew because more growth hormone was demanded and released. It's a supply and demand thing. The greater the struggle, the greater the demand, resulting in a greater release of hormone leading to greater growth.

In another sense, the Due Time Dimension works as a kind of DNA, a genetic code that unlocks learning potential as you struggle. And once again, the return on what you learn will be in direct proportion to the demand of your struggle, if you will give it a chance to work. We call this our "learning curve." And it is why it's so important you know what The Due Time Dimension is. How it works. And what you need to do to bring about the desired results necessary for success in your life.

In the following chapters we will help you do this. We will first define the Due Time Dimension for you, explain it's stages to you, and then take you through it's life changing, step by step process so you can see it work. Then we will help you apply this knowledge to your own Gruntsville experience using personal stories, illustrations, and anecdotes that will tap into your particular learning style so you too can experience the benefits we did.

Our goal in doing this is to help you become the rising star you were created to be by enabling you to become a successful learner. This will help you turn trials into triumphs as you apply like we did, the valuable lessons of Gruntsville.

THE DUE TIME DIMENSION

The Due Time Dimension is a position of struggle in space and time and where process and schedule work together to create a particular outcome or desired result.

The Due Time Dimension consists of two stages: Process and schedule. The process is a series of actions, operations, or changes that occur over time, and leads to a particular ending. And of course the amount of time it takes for these actions, operations or changes to take place is called the schedule.

Now each stage is one complete step in a sequential or recurrent activity within the dimension. Notice the words complete, step, sequential, recurrent, and activity. In other words, each stage involves one or many of a series of activities or lessons that are continuous, connected, extended, and/or recurrent, and which enable or disable growth and development. This means the lessons of Gruntsville are built upon one another in an incremental, progressive fashion, are connected by the Due Time Dimension, can be extended or repeated if necessary, and leads to either ruin or renewal.

In many ways the Due Time Dimension is like the place in space and time where a trapeze artist struggles to stay afloat high in mid air above the crowd. Between the letting go and the grabbing on there is nothing to hang on to but his or her fading momentum. And between the letting go and the grabbing on, there is no turning back.

Each stage of the acrobatic feat is a complete step performed in a sequential or progressive series. Each succeeding act depends on how complete the prior act was performed. Each series of actions performed or in the process of being performed, can be extended or repeated. And it all leads to either renewal or ruin, depending on how well the trapeze artist allows process and schedule to work.

Another way to illustrate how the Due Time Dimension works is with the butterfly. What begins as a caterpillar, a worm-like larva, ends as a butterfly or moth, but only after going through a series of actions, operations, or changes over time.

You see each stage of development is a complete step fulfilled in a sequential manner or brought about through a series of progressive changes. Each successive change or stage of development depends on the completeness of the prior one, can be extended if necessary, and leads to either renewal or ruin, depending on whether you allow process and schedule to work its magic.

If you don't believe this, just free a butterfly from its cocoon before its due time and watch what it does. It won't be able to fly because its wing muscles won't be strong enough to give it lift. Continued, extended, progressive, sequential, and incremental levels of applied resistance over time is necessary in order for it to develop the strength to fly.

In short, the butterfly needs the DNA of the Due Time Dimension to form and function properly. This is the thing that will stir up and set in motion a planned process of growth and differentiation so it can reach its future goal, maximize its potential, and fulfill its purpose.

As Pennsylvania farm boys, we should have recognized the importance and significance of the Due Time Dimension right away. After all, every spring that we planted crops was a lesson in process and schedule.

The corn, oats, wheat, soybean and barley seeds we dropped into the ground was a miniature Gruntsville experience. And a tough one at that, for them and for us. Plowing, seeding, cultivating and harvesting is not an easy task. Nor is it easy to learn. Or always fun to do. But its important and necessary in order for a farmer to fulfill his or her purpose.

And in terms of seeds, I can't imagine it would be easy or fun to be buried alive and left alone to fend for yourself either. Although I'm sure there are some who have figuratively, or even literally for that matter, experienced this feeling.

But the lesson of the seed is the lesson of Gruntsville. On the outside they don't look like much, but they have potential. And the only way to maximize their potential is to bury them. And so we did.

We couldn't see what was happening inside their dark soiled cocoon, but over time, and given the right conditions, they turned their trial into triumph because they allowed the process and schedule of the Due Time Dimension work for them.

Well, I don't know which illustration is more like the Gruntsville you may presently be experiencing but I do know some people right now who very much feel stuck in, or with, a particular painful circumstance. Others who feel very much alone and dormant, buried in dark soil of sorrow and unable to see any light at the end of the tunnel. And I also know of others who are hanging on to nothing but fading momentum in their lives, hoping to grab on to something or some one else because they have been hung out to dry.

I guess my maroon platoon experience was similar to both the butterfly and the seed. I remember my Gruntsville feeling more like a prison than a womb for growth. I remember feeling trapped and helpless inside that maroon jersey. And I remember feeling alone and abandoned, left to fend for myself in the dark soil of my sorrowful circumstances.

And when things didn't go according to plan I quietly wailed inside the woeful walls of my tomb of travail because things were out of control, and I was feeling unjustly served.

I got tired of the daily drudgery. And I hated going to practice. Because no matter how hard I tried, I couldn't catch a break. And I got sick and tired of Paterno's "keep hustling, something good will happen" sermon.

I remember wanting to just give up and quit, especially when it seemed everyone else I knew was having it easier and better than me.

But my Creator knew this. He knew I would enter my cocoon at Penn State with confidence and a great deal of optimism. He knew I would become discouraged when I hit the wall of doubt. And He knew I would need a lift over the wall to get me through. That's when He reminded me of His promise. His promise that said, in due time I would reap the benefits of doing good, if I didn't quit.

It was this promise that renewed my hope and restored my will to daily persevere, to practice, practice, and practice all the good things the coaches told me to do, even if I would never see the benefits.

This was the key to everything. To faithfully persevere at doing good. To keep fighting, hoping, praying, learning, and practicing, in spite of the drudgery, day after day without giving up. Because even though it looked like I was still a miserable maroon platoon caterpillar on the outside, I was gradually changing and growing stronger on the inside. Until I was finally able to break out and fly. To be the man I was designed to be. To carry out my designed function. To make a contribution. To fulfill my mission and purpose in life.

This is the secret of the Due Time Dimension.

And now, looking back, I can tell you the benefits of this place can only be reaped one step at a time. That its timeless truths and secret treasures are revealed in due time and in due course. That the key of knowledge and understanding unlock its gates only when its travelers are teachable, and ready to learn. And that the timetable and process, the combination factors, are different for all who journey through its village streets.

I can tell you that it is not an easy journey. It's not a simple jog. A walk through the park. Or a day at the beach. In fact, it can become awfully painful. Quite stressful. Terribly difficult. And rather perilous at times.

Gruntsville is full of hazards, pitfalls, booby traps, and terrible darkness. And it requires deliberate, cautious, and illumined movements along the way in order to get through it successfully.

In spite of it all however, the journey, the experience, has tremendous benefits for anyone willing to learn its lessons.

How about you? Are you determined to see things through? Are you willing to struggle against the weight of your trials, tragedies, and failures, without giving up? Are you willing to learn the lessons of Gruntsville?

If so, let the games begin as we wind up and deliver you a curve ball with our opening pitch in the next chapter.

THE EAR AND EARN IN LEARN

The return on what you learn in Gruntsville will be in direct proportion to the demand of your struggle and your willingness to let the Due Time Dimension work for you.

Think of it as a curve ball or change up. From the time it is released by a pitcher to the time it reaches the batter an amazing thing happens. It's position in space and time changes due to the release and rotation of the pitcher. In other words, the return on the pitch (ie. success of the pitch) will be in direct proportion to the demand placed upon the seams of the baseball as it struggles (rate of rotation) against air molecules over time and distance. The better the control of rotation, the better the pitch, and the greater the effectiveness. This is an illustration of your Learning Curve. And it's an amazing thing to discover.

Remember the promise I received the night I was ready to quit the Penn State football team? The pitch that said I would reap if I didn't lose heart and quit in doing good? Well, I turned that thing over and over in my mind, day after day, rotating it against the air currents of my struggle until the Due Time Dimension worked its magic using process and schedule to change my position on the team over time.

Jeff and I can tell you, based on our experiences, that the Learning Curve works. That it's true. And that the return on its investment is directly proportional to the demand of your struggle, your willingness to listen--to give ear to its lesson, and the degree to which you allow the Due Time Dimension do its thing.

This is why you need to master its pitch too. Understanding its principle components and how they work together will help you become a successful learner, and ultimately a successful finisher in your Gruntsville marathon.

You see, successful pitching and learning have several things in common. Both require skill. Both demand a teachable attitude. Both have value. And both involve change. All four components are necessary in becoming an effective learner. Or in becoming a successful "anything" for that matter.

Now, skills are abilities or dexterity that comes from training or practice. And whether it's communication or interpersonal, study, or athletic skills, developing them requires deliberate, daily, repetitious use and application. In other words they require practice, practice, practice. And then more practice, and more training, until the skill level is changed. That is, until it becomes mastered. And since it is impossible for an individual to move constructively and productively to higher levels of performance without planned training, it is essential and necessary you plan and implement a personal and professional development program. More on this in our chapter titled "The Mystery of Mastery."

Now a lot has been written about the importance of attitude. It is a mental position or feeling regarding a fact or state. And because it affects the quality and rate of skill acquisition and development, you will need to consider its mastery as well.

I'm sure you're aware of the mind games that are played out in the boardrooms, locker rooms, classrooms and living rooms of the world. So we'll explore this component of learning in our next chapter on mind games. We'll also talk about learning readiness, that is, developing a teachable attitude, we'll cover this in our chapter titled, "Fangs of Futility."

And then values are something having or held to have real worth or merit. Without values, our pursuits, passions, and pride in achievement wouldn't amount to much. In many ways, our beliefs or "core values" if you will, are what drives and motivates us to learn and grow. So we'll talk about this in our chapter on "Perilous Pursuits."

Finally, change is the act, process or result of modifying, reversing, switching, transferring, altering, transforming, varying, or substituting. The maroon platoon cocoon story is a perfect example of the kind of change we're talking about here. Without change I wouldn't have become a starter. Jeff wouldn't have won a Super Bowl, and baseball and learning would not exist. Therefore, since change is inevitable, we must master its use to succeed, because managing change is what success is all about.

You see, life is full of transitions. Change Ups. Also called "off speed" pitches. And they are times when endings become new beginnings, and when new beginnings become endings. Some transitions are expected or anticipated, and others are not. Some are fun, others are misery. Some are easy, others difficult. The point is, you must understand the nature of change and learn how to manage it in order to earn a greater return.

Now most of us encounter transitions with a great deal of unbridled optimism. Both Jeff and I did. Both of us expected to succeed quickly in sports. To move up the ladder of stardom without any set backs or interruptions.

Were they unrealistic expectations? Perhaps. Maybe we should have been more cautious in our approach. But one thing is sure, when unbridled optimism hits the brick wall of reality, doubt sets in. And when this happens, you need some help over the wall. This is where your learning curve kicks in. Where attitude, skills and values help lift you over the wall and on to renewed levels or degrees of optimism and confidence in reaching your goals.

I hit the brick wall of doubt and pessimism when Paterno switched me to defense and put me on the Maroon Platoon. It was a monumental transition I hadn't expected. And at first, I didn't know how to manage the change, how to master the curve ball thrown at me, and because of that I almost struck out. If I hadn't been rescued by the knowledge of the Due Time Dimension I would have gone down swinging.

Instead, the Due Time Dimension reminded me to check, develop, and then add to my present portfolio of attitudes, skills and values. In doing so, it coached me up and over the wall of pessimism and doubt and on to new heights and levels of confidence and success.

This is the Learning Curve's cycle of success. And it's the way to managing change.

Someone once said, "Life is like a ten speed bike, most of us have gears we never use." I agree. When you hit the hill of pessimism and doubt, your going to need to switch into some other gears you may have never used before in order to get up over its summit. You're going to have to change gears in your attitude, skills and values in order to move on to new heights and renewed levels of confidence and success.

That's what Jeff and I did. And in the following chapters we'll tell you about it. We have some stories that will describe and illustrate the kinds of attitudes, skills, and values that are important in reaching your summit of success.

So study this pitch, work on your return, give ear to this lesson, consider adding on to or improving upon your present portfolio of attitudes, skills and values, and allow process and schedule to work its magic. It's a pitch that will K.O. your opponents; a gear that will lift you up and over your wall of doubt in Gruntsville.

LET THE GAMES BEGIN

Joe Paterno and Bill Parcells were masters at playing them. Some players seemed to thrive on them. Others hated them. They're called mind games. And sometimes they worked and sometimes they didn't.

You see, mind games are used to get inside the "psyche", the heart and mind of an individual or team. They're motivational methods and techniques employed by coaches, teachers, employers, and even parents for the purpose of enhancing individual and team performance.

Parcells loved messing with your mind. It was his standard operating procedure for manipulating, provoking, influencing, and to a degree even controlling a player's behavior or performance. As a matter of fact, he became so accustomed to playing mind games that he did it almost unconsciously. And over the years it became his behavioral trademark as he went about tattooing his mental little games on the minds of his players.

Now we told you at the top that sometimes they worked and sometimes they didn't. The result depends on the player's attitude, learning style, and ability to master the inner, mysterious matters of the mind.

Guys like Lawrence Taylor loved Parcell's silly little games. And it seemed to bring out the best in his performance. But it just so happened Parcells' mind game methods were tailored, no pun intended, to L.T.'s learning style. L.T. was a concrete sequential learner. He loved Bill's methods even though they often lacked substance, sense, or an organized, sequential process. However, when Parcells resigned from the Giants and Ray Handley took over as head coach, L.T.'s performance declined, in large part due to Handley's different coaching style. Handley presented his lessons in a logical, sequential, organized, and systematic style that allowed little room for illogical mental horse play.

On the other hand, Parcells' mind games seemed to produce counter results in Jeff's performance. I can remember Jeff telling me how upset and disheartened he became with Parcells when after one of his games as a sidelined, back-up, clipboard toting quarterback, his work was tossed into the trash can by Bill without so much as a glance at it. When Jeff confronted him with what he had done, Parcells simply chuckled, "it was to keep you in the game." Needless to say, that mind game didn't go over very well with Jeff. His learning style preferred lessons of substance, methods that were rational, and sequential in nature in order for him to derive any meaningful use from them. Perhaps L.T. would have enjoyed this game, Jeff deplored it. He needed a different approach, a different method to motivate and thus enhance his performance. Not a one size fits all approach.

Paterno played his mind games too. I'm sure you remember the verbal assault he inflicted on me my first day of practice. Now I'm sure he wanted me to get his point, and I eventually did, but it took a lot of time and struggling on my part to learn it.

You see, I was, and still am an Abstract Random Learner. ARL's are distinguishable by their attention to human behavior and have an extraordinary ability to sense and interpret "vibrations." In other words I am attuned to nuances of atmosphere and mood. I associate the medium with the message. I tie a teacher's manner, delivery, and personality to the message being conveyed. In doing so, I evaluate a learning experience as a whole.

So you can guess how I responded to Paterno and his message. I didn't get it. And so I struggled and struggled until one of our senior team captains gave me some good advice. He told me to listen to what Paterno has to say rather than how he says it.

Only after discussing this with him, and reflecting on his words and my experience as a whole, was I able to move on in my performance. You see my learning style preferred to receive information in a non-threatening manner and required discussion and reflection, that is "soaking time" in order to learn from it. Paterno's impatient, "do it my way or else" one size fits all method of motivating didn't work for me. I needed discussion and reflection time to organize my thoughts and sort out the medium from the message in order to grow as a ball player.

Now I know some of you will say you can't argue against success. After all, Paterno and Parcells are two of the most successful collegiate and professional football coaches of all time. So they must be doing something right. Well you're right. They are doing things right. But you can also make the argument for numbers. That is, if a coach has enough talent on his team, enough meat on the hoof so to speak, then those who don't get it, his way, can and will be replaced by those who do. And believe me, Jeff and I witnessed the demise of a lot of great athletes because of this very fact.

The important thing in all of this is not whether Paterno and Parcells are successful coaches, they are. Or that you need a PHD in learning styles to become successful. Although it could help. The point is, you need to understand the nature and purpose of mind games so you can adjust, learn from them if possible, and then move on so you won't be replaced by someone else. You need to understand the potential and learning capacities of the mind's inner chambers. How it operates, how it can envision, lead, guide, and create. In other words, you need to become a student of learning in order for you to grow personally and professionally.

Paterno used to tell us that "90% of football is played from the neck up." He knew that all other things being equal, the player who best mastered his mind ended up on top. And I think he's right. The mind is the battlefield where the war of Gruntsville takes place. That's why you need to master its use.

It's been said, "The mind is the cabinet of imagination, the treasure of reason, the registry of conscience, and the council chamber of thought." This is important to understand and remember if you are to win the battle for the mind. Your mission therefore, is to arm yourself with this knowledge, otherwise the forces and pressures of head games, negative circumstances, and low resistance will blow you out of the water.

You must struggle to keep your cabinet of imagination alive. And to practice using it often. Because it opens your future to unforeseen possibilities. It's a tool to help you engineer into reality the desired results you wish for.

You see, Disney World was built on imagination. And today, their "Imagineering" exhibition is one of its most popular attractions. Their purpose is to engineer imaginations. That is, to plan and bring into being that which is imagined. Disney understands its nature, its power, its purpose, and its nurturing requirements. You need to do the same, particularly when Gruntsville begins to cloud your vision.

You must also work to maximize your mind's treasure of reason. It helps to explain, justify, and comprehend events, circumstances, and changes when they don't at first make sense. It opens the door of your mind to different and unlimited possibilities and solutions to problems. And you must be careful to keep it sharp and alert with reading, study, investigation, research, and reflection, otherwise the drudgery and difficulty of Gruntsville will tear it down and wear it out.

Now the registry of conscience illumines and lights your way. It's your inner compass to guide you in your choices. Your point of reference when the darkness of disaster and disappointment lures you off course. And it's important you register and document the values and principles you believe in. After all, its been said, "If you don't know what you believe in, you'll fall for anything." And you certainly don't want to fall for, or be lured off course by someone selling you instant results and easy way outs. There's no such thing. They will cost you dearly in the long run.

And finally, the council chamber of thought leads you along the path of understanding. Understanding is an acquisition that is said to be more profitable than silver and yield better returns than gold. That it is more precious than rubies, leads to peace and safety, and that nothing you desire can compare to it.

All four of these dimensions work together as pistons of one engine, and are necessary to keep you on course and moving ahead. Without all four, you will misfire, choke off, and eventually shut down altogether when the mental war games begin.

In another sense, they act as your point man, a company leader, who leads you through the jungles and mine fields of Gruntsville. They arm, instruct and train you along the way. They help you advance by using your attitudes, skills, and values as weapons of warfare. They shield and protect you from the stinging arrows of mind games, and penetrate the confusing darkness of doubt, despair and negative circumstances like a sword.

Imagination, reason, conscience, and thought. Four in one. Your guide, companion and fearless leader in matters of the mind. They are indeed your help in times of trouble.

Jeff and I were fortunate to have such a point man lead us through our little grunt worlds. When mind games turned into war games, we benefited from their lessons because we kept the cabinet of our imagination open, tapped the treasure of our reason, checked in with our conscience, and followed the council of understanding. Without them, we would have continued in our confused, pessimistic downward spiral of despair leading to ruin.

So when the malice of mind games turns your high hopes and high expectations into pessimism and doubt, enlist the help of imagination, reason, conscience and thought. They will point the way for you. They will lift you up, and lead you out to growth, opportunity, and chance.

Listen to these words and learn from their instruction. When the games begin, they will coach you along your track of trials and over the hurdles of doubt and despair, to the finish line of personal and professional success.

PERILOUS PURSUITS

"It was January 1st when I arrived on my first visit to the United States. I turned on the television and saw a picture the like of which I had never seen before. It was a rear-view shot of a row of big men in tight pants bending over in such a fashion that they appeared to be putting intolerable strain on said pants. Behind them stood a man who seemed to have lost his temper completely. He was yelling and shouting, apparently because the other men had his ball and he wanted it back. Eventually, after much shouting, they gave it to him. He promptly gave it to one of his friends who ran a few steps and was treated to an awful beating by some other men wearing similar tight pants, but of a different color.

They were apparently very sorry about their behavior because, after they had beaten him up, they gathered in a small group to pray about it. They were not sincere, however, because they went straight back and did the same thing again.

After repeating this whole outrageous procedure about 10 times, the man with the ball suddenly threw it about 60 years to another man I hadn't noticed before. He caught it, ran a few yards, did a funny little dance, and the crowd went wild. I thought I had stumbled on some religious festival (subsequently I discovered I was right!) and was completely mystified until someone started to explain what was happening so that a newly arrived Englishman could understand.

It appeared that the quarterback had so effectively faked a hand-off to his running back that the defensive line and linebackers had played the run, leaving the receiver wide open to catch the pass and go in for a touchdown. And it all happened because the defensive players pursued the man without the ball."

The author, Stuart Briscoe, concludes this story from his book titled, What Works When Life Doesn't by saying, "The moral of the story is, if you are free to pursue happiness, don't be faked into pursuing it where it isn't!"

Unfortunately, too many people today are getting faked out in life. They're pursuing the man without the ball. The wrong object. The wrong goal.

During the stormy trials of my early NFL career, I came to understand that my pursuit of becoming a successful pro quarterback was secondary to the the pursuit of goals I could stake my life on. Why? Because putting my identity in something of limited value, would only leave me feeling bitter and depressed, unable to handle defeat or injury. I needed to put my identity in, and stake my significance to the God whose value is above anything else. The One who guaranteed to support me whether I succeeded or failed.

I realized the night I knelt at the bedside of my sleeping son that God had a greater purpose for me than becoming a successful NFL quarterback or getting to the Super Bowl. The struggle I was engaged in was being used by God to make my life more useful to Him. And He was trying to use my passion, pride and pleasure and drives toward this end.

You see, too many people spend their entire lives striving to attain positions and achievements. They painstakingly climb the "ladder of success" rung by rung-- the degree, the high-profile company, the late nights, the building of an impressive resume-only to find that when they reach the top, the ladder is leaning against the wrong wall. They achieve what they always wanted, but feel empty. They've been faked out. Their perilous pursuits trapped them into thinking they were going to bring fulfillment and satisfaction.

Now I'm not saying that it is wrong to seek or achieve success or to pursue things that bring pride and pleasure. However, the question they must ask themselves is why they want it. Will it honor God? Will it truly satisfy them? Will it truly fulfill them? Will it truly make a difference in their organization, family, community, and the world?

When you get to the point of pursuing things that really matter, and pay the price of preparation and training that is required to fulfill it, you will find that the positions and achievements will come naturally. And more importantly, you'll find immense satisfaction in leaving a real legacy, not a counterfeit. This is what happened to me. But its a challenge not to get faked out in the process.

What you need is a counter-trap perspective. A good understanding of driving forces of passion, pride, and pleasure. A perspective that will lead you in the right direction and keep you on the right path. One that will keep you from getting trapped--rendering your life useless, meaningless and powerless.

THE COUNTER-TRAP PERSPECTIVE

I'll never forget the conversation I had with Kevin Costner during a dinner party one evening at Trump Plaza in Atlantic City. My Dad and brother Ron were with us as we waited for the start of the World Heavy Weight Championship boxing match between George Foreman and Evander Hollyfield.

Costner turned to me and asked if I heard myself breathing while I was playing on the field during the Super Bowl. I told him I didn't. He then asked me if I felt my heart pounding during the game. Again, I said no, but this time I grew more puzzled by his question. What was he getting at, I wondered. What was he looking for? And a quick glance at my brother Ron, who was standing between us, confirmed my bewilderment. We were both perplexed, as we tried figuring out Costner's questions.

But just then I got it! I understood what he was doing as I glanced back at his face and into his eyes. He had this look. A look as though he were trying to picture himself as a quarterback playing in the Super Bowl. He had gone off into his acting mode, trying to mentally and emotionally grasp a picture of what it was like inside the body and uniform of a Super Bowl quarterback.

What was he doing? He was trying to get perspective--the power or ability to see or think of things in their true relationship with one another.

Don Johnson, the former "Miami Vice" superstar, also wanted to know what it was like to win a Super Bowl. After a dinner he and I both attended at the White House in Washington D.C. he asked me "Well, what was it like?" I said, "What was what like?" He said, "The Super Bowl, what else?"

You see, as an actor and former scholastic football player himself, Johnson was trying to get a true picture, a perspective of the event.

Well, not long after the Foreman/Hollyfield fight, I phoned Ron to ask him if he wanted a picture of Costner and us together. Apparently a photographer for H.B.O. (Home Box Office) had taken some snapshots of us together that evening and later called me to see if I was interested in receiving them. They were supposedly being used for the cover of some tabloid magazines.

"You bet. I'll take one", Ron said. But then I began to chuckle as I told him about the phone call I had received from the photographer. Apparently he didn't know who the guy in the middle of the picture was, so he inked him out. The guy was Ron.

Yea, Ron and I both got a good laugh out of this incident. But you know what? The more I thought about that ink blot, the more I realized this is the way life is going to end for a lot of people who are chasing dreams and using their lives in a way that have very little, if any, meaningful substance or lasting purpose.

You see, I know lots of people who live for moments like these. Limousine escorts, private dinners with the President, conversations with Hollywood mega-stars, world renown fame, riches and power. But you know what? Having or doing all these things doesn't make a life. Jesus warned the people of His day to "Watch out! Be on your guard against all kinds of greed; a man's life does not consist in the abundance of his possessions." (Luke 12:15).

What's He really saying here? He is saying that we need to be careful to bridle our passion, pride and pleasure drives. They are powerful motivators in our lives that surge to the surface in our attitudes and actions, and unless we control them, will lead to destructive ends.

In themselves, all three are both good and necessary. And each plays a vital role in our drive for significance. But none can truly bring fulfillment apart from our Creator. He designed us this way.

You see, passion helps drive us to procreate and rule in our world. And we were created to use this God given energy to organize and lead our world for good. Passion enables us to provide, gather in, gain satisfaction from productive work, and enjoy the fruit of our labor. But it was never intended to focus on ourselves. Its intent is to contribute to God's glory, not our own. Left to itself, it will run wild and rough shod. This is what greed is and does. It's a driving appetite for wanting more than you need. It's the passion to possess. The desire or longing for more. And it can become a monster if you don't understand and master its use.

Now pride is an inner force which drives us to establish, protect, enhance, and maintain our self-worth. It serves to guard and promote our significance at all cost. And to be properly managed, pride must hear the counsel of God. For its been said we were not made for ourselves, but were created for God. Not understanding this leads to disaster, like the old saying, "pride precedes a fall."

Pleasure is another God-intended thing. It's been said that man's chief end is to glorify God and enjoy Him forever. Our search for pleasure drives us in much of what we are and do. Pursuing pleasure is not wrong if it brings glory to God.

So you see, these things are not bad in themselves. But if you're not careful, the greedy ghoul of Gruntsville will seduce you into seeking your significance elsewhere. And isn't this what your Gruntsville quest is all about anyway? Seeking importance in life?

Remember our introduction? We described Gruntsville as a little place where little people did little things with there lives. And they wanted out because they wanted to be big people doing big things in big places. Well, the driving forces of passion, pride and pleasure are good motivations to get you out of there, but you must be careful not to let them run wild and rough shod in your pursuit of success. Apart from God, they lead to the ink blot of futility and meaninglessness.

REALITY BITES

I remember a story once told about an island of natives that one day went out and picked up a bunch of writing pens that had been dropped from a passing plane. Not knowing their function or intended purpose, they used them to dig pits out of grapefruit.

Unfortunately, it seems a lot of people on the island of Gruntsville are using their lives in a similar manner. Not knowing their real function and intended purpose they are using the driving forces of passion, pride, and pleasure to dig pits out of grapefruit. To dig out of the pit they are in. But it won't work. The pit, the empty feeling in your soul cannot be dug out of by misusing these God given drives. Apart from God they will only lead to the monster of more. More longing, more digging, and more futility. The only way to fill this money pit, this monstrous black hole of more, is by getting more of God Himself. After all, He designed this way. He created us with this inner pit for more in order for us to be driven to Him.

I'll be the first to tell you this is the way things are. Apart from God, money, fame and power won't satisfy the quest for significance. It will only lead to the ink blot of futility when reality bites.

And when is that? At what time and in what place will reality bite you? Perhaps its bitten you now in Gruntsville. Perhaps Gruntsville's been a wake-up call for you. Time for you to consider your purpose and destiny in life. Time for you to gain a different perspective as you look at the ink blot you'll be left with at the end of your days if you don't make any changes right now.

So consider the significance of this lesson as you consider your drive for significance. Take a snapshot of what your life will be like at the end of your days if you continue pursuing the things you are. What does it look like?

Take a moment to let the light of God's truth and the Due Time process develop a good life picture for you. Consider His picture of success. Get a perspective from His angle. Then shoot away. Create a picture album with your life that will positively influence generations to come. This way, when reality bites, it will bite into the picture of a living legacy, not undeveloped film.

THE MYSTERY OF MASTERY

What if we told you the secret to climbing your way out of Gruntsville lies under your feet and on top of your head? Would you know what we're talking about or what to look for?

And would you believe us if we told you the measure of success you experience in your climb will depend greatly on your ability to master this mystery?

Well, climbing out of Gruntsville is a mystery that requires mastery and you can master the mystery by simply tapping your feet and your mind's treasure of reason.

No, this isn't something out of "Wizard Of Oz." We're not saying you can escape the clutches of Gruntsville's wicked witch of the west by simply tapping your heels together and repeating "There's no place like home." If only it were that simple.

We are simply saying you need to wisely think through the nature of your climb before you attempt to scale its treacherous, slippery slopes. You need to consider the quality, character, and constitution of your steps because their placement will determine the amount and extent of time and energy it is going to take you, and the degree of satisfaction and fulfillment you experience in getting there.

How do we know? Just call it first hand climbing experience. An experience that began when we were just kids, facing daily, the challenge, adventure, and mystery of mastering a particular hill on our farm. A hill that in one sense was a mini-Gruntsville for us, and in another sense our stairway to success once we mastered the climb.

You see, step-by-step, day-by-day, we would climb and descend this oak timbered slope because Dad told us to. And we called it "Dad's Wooden Hill" because he was the one in charge, the one who scheduled our daily climbs.

Now this ramped ritual was actually passed down to us through the generations. It was a persistent practice derived from our descendants, an exercise inherited from our ancestors. And to be honest, we often got tired of Dad's daily detail, missing altogether the point of this special duty.

Now this hill is similar to, but different from most hills you might climb in Western Pennsylvania. It's slope is relatively steep but safe. It's lined with strong, sturdy oak timbers, and can generally be scaled anytime, night or day. Although the terrain isn't rocky or strewn with fallen timbers, there were times we tripped and lost our footing because we were in too great a hurry. But thankfully we were able to catch ourselves or soften our fall by grabbing on to the hand rail next to us. It was constructed back when the trail was blazed, and the skin of its bark wears a smooth glow from years and years of steady use.

Now, looking back over all those days and years of climbing and descending, we can appreciate the experience, the mystery surrounding it, and the lesson it taught us. The lesson of mastery.

You see, this hill was the staircase in our old farmhouse that connected the living room to the second floor bedrooms. It was our means of getting to and from two separate and distinctive, yet meaningful and purposeful places. Places that were different but significant in form and function.

Every morning we descended Dad's Wooden Hill to the story below, to do our chores, perform in school and sports, and apply ourselves to the disciplines of life. And every night we ascended it to the story above, anxious to rebuild, restore, and renew our dreams, our hopes, and our wearied lives.

Two stories, different levels, different functions, and yet connected by treads and risers that symbolized life's staircase to success.

Like most people, we were always in a hurry to climb the ladder of success. Always in a hurry to get to the next level, the next chapter in the story of our lives. We couldn't wait for the day we could start varsity, graduate from high school, and leave the drudgery of farm life to seek fame and fortune for ourselves. And the way we traveled up and down Dad's Wooden Hill reflected this. I'm sure we spent too much time and energy thinking about the day's events, anticipating what was going to happen, and reflecting on what had happened, always looking forward or backward, living in the past or projecting into the future, never pausing long enough to think about the mystery right under our feet or to learn from it.

But that's the great thing about Gruntsville. Its misfortunate circumstances, trials and tribulations have a way of stopping us in our tracks, tripping up our plans, frustrating our progress, and knocking us off stride. In short, its a wake-up-call to master the mystery of climbing before you attempt to master the hill.

Now some people seem to have a knack for mastering mysteries. Like Sherlock Holmes they approach mysteries with a determined, deliberate, step by step plan. They collect information, gather data, pay attention to details, ask questions, surmise possibilities and hypothesize solutions. The knowledge they acquire is then put to test through a series of actions to prove their theories right or wrong.

In a similar way we need to tap into our treasure of reason before we move our feet. We need a step by step plan to master the mystery of Gruntsville before we attempt to climb out of it. We need to acquire knowledge about it first, and then put that knowledge to work. In doing so, our understanding increases, we make better decisions and we experience greater success.

Let's go back to the maroon platoon cocoon for a moment. Mastering the mystery of the cocoon is a prerequisite to mastering the climb out. The step by step transformation process that occurs inside the cocoon needs to be understood in order to allow patience, perseverance and hard work to pay off. Without the knowledge of the cocoon, people lose heart and quit before its "due time" has a chance to work.

So this is the reason we need to recognize, acquire, and apply important knowledge about the character and constitution of our steps. It leads to mastery. And because mastery can only be achieved and experienced on a cumulative basis, that is, one step, one lesson at a time, it's important you take a moment right now to consider its incremental value and ultimate worth as you attempt to climb out of your Gruntsville.

You see, a staircase is built with steps. And each step is composed of treads and risers. Treads are the horizontal parts we set foot on, and the risers the upright members between them. As a whole, they work together to allow ascendancy and descendancy over a wide range of heights and distances. Without them, we would not be able to get from one level to another in our homes.

In a similar way, the lives we build require treads and risers to reach our goals. The risers are knowledge and the treads are understanding. They work together to allow us to move from one level to another, and over a wide range of heights and distances in our careers and personal pursuits. The treads and risers of knowledge and understanding work together by incorporating both knowing and doing. It means tapping our treasure of reason by using our intellect and senses to gather and synthesize information, and then tapping our feet, putting that information to work. One without the other is simply futility. You have got to have both to reach the top. And that is why paying attention to your daily steps is so critical to reaching your goal and getting to the next level in your life plan.

Now most people try to climb the ladder of success without much if any patience, and without much if any regard for "treading out" their knowledge. That is, they don't put wings to their faith, their ideas into action, or allow the mystery of mastery to work its magic because they're always in too great a hurry. All they want is to get to the top as quickly and effortlessly as possible. To squeeze from the fruit of succulent success all the juice that they can, as fast as they can, with as little work as they can, even before its been given a chance to ripen.

But what happens? In their attempt to cut corners and take short cuts, to hurry along the fruit before it's ready, they sacrifice quality for patience, taste for time.

And so it is with the lives we build. Too many people are sacrificing taste for time. They are cutting corners, taking short cuts, and skipping steps on their way up the success stairway only to discover something still missing in their lives. What they are left with is the sour aftertaste of unripened fruit. And it all happens because they fail to seek the secret under their steps. They fail to understand the mystery of mastery.

You see, mastery requires daily application of knowledge. In other words lots and lots of treading out information. Without the 'treading" there is no understanding. And without understanding, there is no rise in elevation. Your position, purpose, and potential remain flat. You experience activity, not progress, motion without movement.

Another word for mastery is overlearning. It simply means repeating, rehearsing, and practicing until the thought, attitude or behavior is overcome or becomes automatic. And this is accomplished as each riser of knowledge and every tread of understanding is touched and put to work on the practice field of everyday life.

Yes, mastery requires daily, repetitious, purposeful, and disciplined stepping. Putting to task and to test the attitudes, skills, and values of life's daily drudgeries. It demands each step of knowledge be treaded out in the routine, daily practices of personal and professional life until it becomes a habit of understanding. And then, and only then, will you experience the full measure of success.

Again, you can try puddle jumping over some of the treads. Especially the ones that seem insignificant or useless. But in the end, your impatience and hurriedness will catch up to you. Because even though you may reach the top sooner, the treads you skipped in the process will show up in your character and in your work. You will have scaled to the summit of incompleteness, later realizing that each tread had been a prerequisite, a necessary lesson of labor needed for building into your soul the glorious goal of contentment and completeness.

John Wooden, the legendary basketball coach of the U.C.L.A. Bruins during their 1970's NCAA Championship reign, understood the magnificence of mastery. He knew the value and wisdom of patient, step by step skill acquisition. He knew how to develop complete players. He developed a coaching model called "pyramid of success" that builds specific skills and character traits on top of one another until the goal of mastery is achieved.

In a similar fashion, each tread and riser of Dad's Wooden Hill represented a lesson to be learned, a value to be internalized, or a test to be passed in order to achieve rise towards our goal. The steps Dad put us through on the farm, the challenges and chores, the demands and the drudgery, were his way of treading out in us the knowledge we had acquired. In other words, the farm was a daily lesson in problem solving. Of putting knowledge into action, belief into behavior, one step, one lesson at a time.

In his own sort of way he was teaching us the lesson of the staircase. That treading needs to be progressive, incremental, and sustained, in order for us to receive maximum elevation in our climb. Without this lesson, we would probably have become empty finishers. Puddle jumpers. Winners of want rather than winners of worth. Having everything, becoming nothing. Reaching the finish line of futility rather than the finish line of fullness.

No, Grunts don't turn into rising stars by cutting corners or puddle jumping over difficult steps . They are transformed one step, one lesson, one thought, one attitude, one behavior at a time.

So stop for a moment to consider the mystery under your feet. Master it. Then master the hill before you. It's the only way to climb the stairway to success.

THE DOGS OF DRUDGERY

Enter Gruntsville and you will soon be hunted down by the Dogs of Drudgery. You'll be hounded daily by some of the most menial, difficult, common, ordinary, tiresome, and dirty work imaginable.

Drudgery is every day grub work. It's the daily routine with its common everyday tasks. It's doing little stuff, in little places, that seemingly goes unnoticed. And it's stuff we would just rather not do. We would rather do big stuff, in big places, in front of big people.

I remember well.

You see, the Dogs of Drudgery tracked me down inside the gate of my maroon platoon on the very first day. They growled and nipped at my heels as I went about my training in Gruntsville's dirty little trenches. And they never seemed to stop as I tried to faithfully perform my maroon platoon duties.

But I hated my tour of duty in this miserable jungle. I just couldn't stand the menial, tiresome tasks I had to perform in practice. And to make matters worse, I never received any recognition for my service. I had to sit in the stands or stand on the sidelines while the starters got to play in a big stadium, in front of big audiences, for big time rewards. In other words, they got to howl from the mountain tops while I whimpered like a puppy from my sideline prison. Doesn't really seem fair, does it?

Well, I didn't **think** so.

And as a result of **thinking** this way, my vision for what I could be faded, my treasure of reason declared bankruptcy, my registry of conscience closed the book on me, and my understanding took a nose dive. So I pulled back in my effort and quit trying as hard as I used to. I began cutting corners in my training and found myself always looking around to see if the coaches were watching me when I did.

You see, that was my way of getting even with the coaches and their system of doing things. After all, if they weren't going to recognize my efforts or reward my hard work with a promotion to the first team, then I wasn't about to over exert myself on things that wouldn't matter or make a difference.

So every practice I just went through the motions. Gradually giving up and getting worse in the process.

What I didn't know or understand at the time was, I was not only hurting my team but I was also hurting myself. Every practice that I went through the motions, a piece of me seemed to die inside. My pride, self-respect, and work ethic disintegrated little by little, until I hit rock bottom. Once there, my only escape seemed to be quitting.

All along, I quit listening to, and believing in Paterno's principle that said, "Keep hustling something good will happen", and "You either get better or worse, you never stay the same." Looking back, I could have prevented a lot of heart ache, and head ache, if I had applied this principle sooner than I did.

But this is the way Gruntsville is. The schedules for learning its lessons are different for each of us who journey through its gates. And my stop at this gate took a little longer than it probably should have. Although I finally did make it through.

You see, I needed to get to the point where I no longer saw my grunt work as insignificant. I had to come to the realization that little things matter. That those who prove themselves steady, firm, and dependable in the little things, will prove themselves in the big things. And that this kind of unswerving, unwavering, dependable attitude isn't developed over night. It takes lots and lots of practice, training, and drudgery to accomplish it.

Now most people believe training and development are important for success. But they don't always act this way.

I sure didn't. I first believed in them, but when I didn't see instant results or gain immediate, observable growth, I lost heart and almost quit altogether.

Perhaps you have experienced this too. Perhaps you have the dogs of drudgery nipping at your heels, waiting to see if you muzzle them by getting better or become their next dinner by falling at their feet.

No, getting better isn't easy. But it's necessary because the vast majority of people know full well that without continuous growth, the very best player, employee, or performer of today will be outdated quickly. That's precisely why all of us need to give careful consideration to getting better at what we do. We either get better or worse, we never stay the same.

You see, over the years, several beliefs regarding individual and professional growth have persisted. One of these is, of course, the belief that we need to get help in the areas of perceived need or opportunity. We look for ways to convert a weakness to a strength, or seek training which makes advancement possible. Another belief which has persisted in one that advocates developing to the maximum our specific areas of interest and our professional strengths. Here, the emphasis has been to put our weaknesses or deficiencies on the back burner while focusing on our proven strengths and abilities. After all, we make our living off what we can do, not what we can't do. And there are many highly successful people, in a variety of fields, who have found success by following one or the other of these paths. However, neither is perfect.

For example, before we get help for our weaknesses, we may have to overcome several obstacles. First, we may not think, or be willing to admit for that matter, that we have any shortcomings. Second, we may get defensive if someone suggests we do. And third, an admission of a shortcoming is often viewed as a weakness too, so why do that? So you see, all of these responses create a dilemma which can put out the fire for professional growth.

That's why the beliefs we hold regarding training and development are very important. We need to get over the idea that we can stay the way we are without any fallout. And that training and development is only for those who are weak.

But make no mistake, training is the single most important ingredient in achieving individual and professional success and acquiring control over our own lives. It's simply impossible for anyone to move constructively and productively to higher levels of performance without planned training.

In his book "Thriving on Chaos, Tom Peters says that training is so vitally important to the individual as well as the organization that it should be mandated in all organizations. He says if we intend to be the best-run organization, it's imperative that training, in service, staff development, and individual growth occur. Sounds like Paterno doesn't he?

Well I should have seen the importance of this back on the farm. All along, I thought hauling manure, gathering eggs, bailing hay, feeding the cows, and filling the silo, was tiresome, boring, tedious, monotonous, dirty work. And most of the time it was. But it had a magic about it. A secret power that seemed to cleanse my heart and mind from the hidden poisons of arrogance, rebellion, selfishness, and unbridled pride.

It had a way of developing a humble attitude of service, a teachable spirit, and a desire to make a contribution. Like we said before, life on the farm was a great lesson in problem solving. And what we discovered through common, menial, ordinary, difficult, tiresome, everyday tasks, was the principle of training.

Someone once said, "Drudgery is the touchstone of character." In other words it is one of the finest tests to determine the genuineness of moral excellence. No one is born either naturally or supernaturally with character; it must be developed. Nor are we born with habits--we have to form virtuous habits with the help of God.

This takes training. And the Bible is full of references for training. In the New Testament it says "Everyone who competes in the games goes into strict training." And the reason they do it is to get ready. To condition and prepare for a test or contest.

Well, the dogs of drudgery were there in Gruntsville to test more than the attitudes, skills, and values I was developing for success. They were testing my moral fortitude, my character. And all along, the training that I hated, was helping to form in me virtuous habits that I love.

This is why drudgery is built into the difficulties of Gruntsville. It's there to test your mettle. It's there to test the material or substance out of which you're made.

Some say sports builds character, others say it reveals it. Sounds to me like it's a little of both. But the real story is training. Without training, you wouldn't have the means of developing your character or assessing its growth.

So stop for a moment and look around. What kind of work have you been avoiding lately because it seems insignificant, hard, menial, tiresome, and useless?
Maybe it's weight lifting, or exercising and conditioning. Perhaps it's picking up after yourself, or doing the laundry. Cooking, cleaning, or maintaining the car. It could be the little stuff or busy work passed on to you by your boss or teacher. All those monkeys he or she has dumped on you, that seem trivial, useless, and purposeless. And of course it could be school work, house chores, or the monotonous, routine drills your coach puts you through at practice.

Have you pulled back in your effort? Have you been just going through the motions. Do you truly believe you know all you need to know to hold on to your job today and tomorrow? That you can stay just as you are until the day you can retire?

If so, you're not alone. And there is a way through it.

Before you digress down this discouraging road of drudgery any further, or decide to give up and quit altogether, consider the importance of this lesson. Apply its truth to your Gruntsville experience. Begin some planned training. Start taking care of the little things, and watch the big things eventually take care of themselves. Be steadfast, constant, reliable, firm, and dependable in the small things, and after a while you will discover that you either get better or worse, you never stay the same.

Remember, training is a tool for you to use to bring about the flesh and blood reality of character in your life. If used wisely, it will ultimately unearth in you a moral excellence unsurpassed in value and beauty. A race worthy to be run.

And oh, as if I didn't have to remind you, the dogs of drudgery will be there to test you, nipping at your heels every step of the way.

Something was wrong. Dead wrong.

The sirens signaled an emergency. They screamed danger. They battered against my eardrums, alerting my senses, sending a cold shiver down my spine.

Standing in our yard, I watched them pass. An ambulance and police cruiser racing down the country road to a point not far beyond our house.

Death had stung our rural community. It had come unannounced and uninvited. On a sunny, warm day under a clear, blue Pennsylvania sky, a friend of mine became the unlucky winner in Mother Nature's cruel game of chance--he was hit by a car. A young, unsuspecting boy who had been riding his bike along our narrow country road.

In the blink of an eye the light in his life was snuffed out. The car that hit him had run off the road. The impact was so great that it rifled him out of his shoes. He was gone in an instant. Never to return again.

Later, after everything was over, I walked down to the scene of the accident, at the curve in the road where he was hit, and stood there horrified as I stared at his blood stained tennis shoe that lay in the grass along the berm. It was a lasting reminder of the sting of death, and the frailty and brevity of human life.

But, it wasn't over. It was just the beginning. For me anyway.

It was the beginning of a long, difficult, and painful journey for me as I tried making sense of it all. As if a ten year old kid really could.

Most of what I remember were the sleepless nights and dreadful days that followed. Nights and days obsessed with the fear of dying.

And questions. I had so many questions.

What happens when you die? Where do you go? Does it hurt? Is there really a heaven and a hell? Why him? Why now? What about me?

I tried earnestly to comprehend this dimension of life, but the explanations I received from my parents, Sunday school teacher, and pastor, didn't entirely relieve my worried heart or conquer my fears.

Before all of this happened, neither death, nor God, had been much of a reality to me. I believed in them as ideas, but they weren't real to me. I had spent most of my time in church playing silly little games to pass the time. I was bored with, and disinterested in theology and church doctrine. They didn't seem to make much sense in my little world of fun and games.

So to pass the time in church I would sleep, play tic-tac-toe, make paper airplanes and shoot spit balls with my friends in the back row. And in summer, when things really got hot and boring, I would look for and occasionally catch a big old horsefly to have some fun with as it came buzzing through the long screenless windows. I would pull some thread from my socks or shirt, tie it around the poor thing's leg, and then let it go. Now and then one would wing its way toward the pulpit, distracting the crowd and pestering the pastor.

Well, this was my way of passing the time and getting out the message that I was bored and wanted to go home. And it often reminded me of the airplanes that flew up and down the Atlantic coast beaches with their trailing banners flapping in the wind. It sure got peoples' attention.

My message was clear alright. And since I didn't understand the message God was trying to get to me I chose to play silly, little games to pass the time.

But you know what? God has a way of getting our attention when we're too busy playing silly little games to pass the time. He has a way of using events and circumstances to wake us up from, and shake us out of, our mindless pursuits, and restore our spiritual acuity. That's what he did to me. And that's what he does through Gruntsville.

You see, death and God did not become a reality to me until the sirens blew and the reaper visited our little country village that fateful Saturday morning. That was my wake-up call. A call to sit up, shake the cob webs from my head and pay attention. A time to begin making sense of my life, and the message God was trying to deliver.

That event made me think about things above and beyond my own little existence. Things like purpose, meaning, and fulfillment. And how to achieve them. I needed someone above and beyond my limited world to help me make sense of things. Because I sure couldn't. No matter how hard I tried, I wasn't capable of taking the sting out of death. I wasn't capable of delivering myself from the fear of dying. I wasn't capable of creating life beyond the grave, or bridging the gap between heaven and hell.

This is what the circumstances of Gruntsville does. It brings you to a point of frustration and despair. It wakes you up to the reality that there are things in life that you can't control and are unable to do. Like delivering yourself for instance. You get to a point where no matter how hard you try, you are unable to save yourself from the mess your in. Unable to gain any meaning or fulfillment in your life or from your work. Unable to gain any measure of lasting peace and satisfaction in the world. And so you look outside yourself to other things or places for deliverance.

This can be good or bad, depending on where you turn for help.

When my semi-conscious brother sat on the sidelines during Super Bowl XXV he turned to smelling salts for help after taking a vicious hit by Leon Seals. It was to keep him from going unconscious. To help him shake out the cobwebs from his head, restore his mental acuity, and get him back in the game.

Years before, when his professional football career took a severe hit, rendering him semi-unconscious on the sidelines as a backup quarterback, he turned to the smelling salts of God's promises to bring him and his career back. It was a crucial move on his part. And it worked. But it worked because he turned in the right direction at the right time and toward the right thing when the knockout punches were delivered.

You see, these knockout moments in life are called turning points. They are life's most crucial places, and lead to either renewal or ruin depending on where and who you turn to for help.

Again, they are like the trapeze artist I told you about earlier. As he swings high above the crowd and lets go of one bar to seize another, he hangs in the air with nothing but his fading momentum. And between the letting go and the grabbing on, there is no turning back.

Gruntsville is full of turning points like this. They're places where you find yourself being either lulled to sleep by near sighted images of success, or knocked out of the real game of life by its devastating hits.

I experienced both in my Gruntsville. There were times I needed smelling salts to regain my acuity and times I almost fell asleep by playing silly little games to relieve my anxiety and pass the time.

Falling asleep reminds me of a true story I once heard about a football player who did just this. In the corner of the locker room before a big game he fell asleep and didn't awake until the players returned after the game was over. You can be sure he regrets that he did.

And in similar fashion, I saw too many people on the maroon platoon sleep their careers and lives away by playing silly little games to pass the time, rather than pursuing or doing the right thing. Rather than pursuing and applying the principles and precepts of God to their careers and their lives. Instead, they played games like, "the one who dies with the most toys wins", "life is short, play hard", "live for the moment", "be your won boss", and " the law of the jungle."

But you know what? I didn't see it help any of them.

These silly little games deceived them into thinking they were looking in the right direction, doing the right thing, at the right time. But they weren't. They were missing the real message while sleeping through the most meaningful game of their lives.

You see, their silly little games tell you the one who dies with the most toys wins. But what they don't tell you is he still dies. And they don't tell you what happens then?

They tell you life is short so play hard. But they don't tell you how to make a life, or what a worthwhile life really consists of.

They tell you to be your own boss. In other words, to do your own thing, when you want, how you want, no matter what. But what they don't tell you is where selfishness and open rebellion really leads to in life.

And then they tell you that in order to survive in this world you have to play according to the law of the jungle. Get them before they get you. Trust no one and take no prisoners.

But what they don't tell you is this kind of thinking will knock you out of the real game of life. It will render you unconscious and useless in your pursuit of a truly purposeful and meaningful life. And when the game clock of your life runs out, you'll be left with nothing but empty despair to embrace. Having lived for nothing more than empty, meaningless pursuits.

Are you at a turning point in Gruntsville? A feeling of being out of sorts and out of place. A place where you seem to be dangling on nothing but fading momentum?

Have you experienced the semi-conscious affects of Gruntsville's vicious, knock out punches? The feeling of losing control while overwhelming darkness blankets your mind?

If so, where have you turned for help? Have you turned to the smelling salts of God's principles to shake out the cob webs and restore your mental and spiritual acuity or have you chosen to play silly little games to pass the time and suppress your anxiety?

Remember, God has a way of getting your attention because He cares about your destiny. He wants to deliver you from Gruntsville's devastating hits and silly little slumbering games. He wants you to experience purpose, meaning and fulfillment in life.

But it's not going to be easy. Life's transitions are difficult and painful. And it's going to require the smelling salts of God's word to see you through them successfully. Turning in His direction is the only way to regain your mental and spiritual acuity, keep you in the game, on your feet, and doing what you do best. Winning at the right things in life.

"Trust in the Lord with all your heart and lean not on your own understanding;in all your ways acknowledge him, and he will make your paths straight."
Proverbs 3:5

THE NOAH PRINCIPLE

I was home from Penn State on Spring break, watching the Mr. Universe contest on television. And I needed some visual motivation to "bulk up", since coach Paterno switched me from quarterback to linebacker. So I tuned into the program.

But while I was turning on and tuning in, my brother Doug was tuning up.   For his senior prom, that is.

After an invigorating shower, shave, and shampoo, he went to his room, and clicked on the electric hair dryer expecting an uninterrupted fluff and dry. But what he got was an electrifying crimp and curl. Not from the hair dryer, but from me.

You see, setting off his hair dryer upstairs, set me off downstairs. My television screen went bizzerk the moment he turned on that menacing, meddling machine. I couldn't see or hear a thing due to the interference it was causing in the television set. So I yelled upstairs for him to turn it off immediately. But there was no response. I yelled again, threatening him this time with a "I'm warning you." But again, there was no response.

Enough was enough. I sprang from my chair, sprinted across the living room, triple-jumped up the stairs, and bolted through his bedroom door. There he sat. Across the room on the edge of his bed, with his head down, and the hair dryer blazing.

I was in his face in an instant. But after glancing up at me for a moment, and without saying a word, he just dropped his head and continued fanning. Obviously he didn't get my point. So I gave it to him. I stuck out my index finger, pointed it directly at his nose, and said some things I shouldn't have.

He looked up at me again. But this time, staring directly into my eyes, he said, "touch me, I dare you, just touch me."

So, I touched him.

When I did, it was like setting off a keg of gun powder. The sparks flew. He exploded into me, knocking me back against the bedroom wall. Surprised, and a little shaken, I grabbed on to him and threw him back across the room against the other wall. Before we knew it, we were out the door, at the top of the stairs, still locked in combat.

I took him to the floor with a one leg take down. His counter move pushed both of us over the edge of the stairs and down the steps. We rolled over the bannister, and landed in the middle of the living room floor. Both clutching on to one another in a death grip.

Mom screamed for the girls to go get Dad, saying, "they're killing each other, they're killing each other." But even he couldn't stop us after showing up on the scene. Although he made several attempts to break us apart by using himself as a human battering ram, he recoiled each time in frustration and pain. Cracking a rib in the process. One of us had apparently nailed him with an elbow. I think it was Doug.

But then a mysterious thing happened. Just when I had my little brother where I wanted him, I heard my Dad say something that stopped me in my tracks. He said, "I dare you two to get over here right now and put your hand on this Bible."

I couldn't believe my ears. But it was true. I turned towards my Dad who was now standing over our big white family Bible that he had placed on the living room floor.

His eyes told me what his heart couldn't say. His insides were being torn apart by our brutality. And he did the only thing a father or mother can do when things like this happen. Intercede by praying and looking for a way to stop the fighting and to repair the hurt.

I immediately sensed I was wrong as my registry of conscience went to work. A cloak of remorse covered me and I felt compelled to follow through on Dad's invitation.

So I let go. I let go of my anger and my brother, to kneel beside my father. And in a matter of moments, all three of us were kneeling beside one another. No longer locked in combat, but in a forgiving embrace.

Reconciliation is really an act of freedom. It allows you to move onward and outward in your relationships by settling past arguments and disagreements that have the potential of shackling your growth and performance. You see, anger turned inward leads to depression. And unreconciled misdeeds can turn a healthy heart into a bitter, resentful, diseased one. Leading to future incapacitation. It will deprive you of your God given capacity or power to overcome and disable you to perform effectively.

Jeff and I have witnessed this phenomenon many times. We've seen ball players with great potential fall by the wayside because they did not reconcile past hurts. They allowed things to fester inside until it disabled them, eventually crippling their capacity to perform.

And not just ball players. But parents and children, husbands and wives, employers and employees, who all too often allowed misdeeds and past hurts to go unreconciled, leaving them emotionally disabled, and crippled in their capacity to perform.

It happened to a sixth grade student I once knew. I remember him experiencing great anxiety and difficulty in school. Not just in class, but with everyone and everything around him. He seemed to carry around a great deal of anger inside. And I had a hunch I knew what it was. So I asked him one day how things were at home. He didn't say a word. I asked him if he was angry at someone at home? Perhaps his mom? Again, he didn't say a word as he sat in his chair with his eyes fixed on the floor. Then I asked him about his dad? I immediately sensed I had hit the nerve center of his anger. He clenched his jaw, knuckled his hands into fists, and angrily spouted, "I hate my dad." I asked why? He said, "because he beat my mom."

Now that young man was having a horrible nightmare in Gruntsville. Things were out of control and unraveling fast in his miserable little world. He was stuck in a cocoon of despair. Unable to resolve his anger and hostility, he began to experience the ugly, and depressing affects that followed. His performance in school declined. He picked fights with others while others picked on him. His appearance grew worse. His health worsened. And eventually he got to the place where the only way out seemed to be quitting. Giving up on everyone and everything else, even himself.

Gruntsville is like this. It's a place where trying times can get the best of people, leading to despair, decline, and death. Maybe not physically, but emotionally, mentally, socially, and spiritually.

If and when it does, I hope you remember to let go. To let go of your anger. Let go of your hurt. Unlock your vengeful grip, take a knee, and embrace the transforming power of reconciliation like my brother and I did. It will get you through the worst of times. The worst of people. And the worst of yourself.

It eventually did for the young student I just told you about. His name is Noah. And I was thrilled to be part of his recovery. He went on to discover and personally experience the amazing, life changing power and benefits of forgiveness. The inner freedom that's gained when you just let go.

You can experience this too by remembering the Noah Principle as you journey through Gruntsville. Just pause at the gate of reconciliation, release the adversaries you hold in your heart, and experience its transforming power as you pass through it. It's the prescription gate to health and well being. The medication for peak performance. A principle to live by, and the liberty bell of personal freedom. So let it ring.

To forgive is to set a prisoner free and to later discover the prisoner was you.

The room seemed to swirl around like a lazy dust cloud as he collapsed upon his cot. He was losing it. Fast.

His counselor took one look at his ankle, turned, and ran out the door. Only to return moments later with the camp nurse. She removed a sharp object from her emergency kit, and painfully criss- crossed his flesh with its cutting jaws. "What was happening?", he thought, as he struggled to maintain consciousness.

Only moments before he had been running and jumping and having a good time with his cabin buddies. Hiking the trail to Big Rock and exploring the deep dark secrets of the hidden caves.

But in his attempt to beat his friends there, to come in first, he took a short cut. He left the trail and leaped from a boulder into some brush, stopping only for a moment to check the ankle he had punctured, supposedly from the sticks and underlying brush.

But it wasn't from sticks. It was from the fangs of a deadly Timber Rattlesnake concealed beneath the sticks and leaves.

On the way to the hospital he asked his counselor if he was going to die. They had the look of fear on their faces. And although they tried to reassure him he wasn't, the blood that was being siphoned from his body by two rubber suction cups seemed to whisper otherwise.

Weeks later, he was to discover the truth.

The den of venomous snakes he had thrust his foot into almost took his life, and his leg.

The doctors, upon his arrival at the hospital, informed the camp nurse they did not have any anti-serum to immediately treat him with, and would have to fly some in from the closest city hospital. The delay almost cost him his life.

And even though the serum they eventually treated him with stabilized his condition, it could do nothing for the gangrene that began to appear two days later. The doctors called his mom and dad for permission to immediately amputate his leg.

All the while, this little nine year old kid didn't know what was going on. Nor did he comprehend the seriousness of the situation. He only knew, he was awfully sorry for taking that short cut.

After confiding with their family physician back home, his mom and dad decided against the doctors' request to immediately remove their little boy's leg. He was given one more night to improve. In the morning, it was either his leg, or his life, the doctors said. His mom and dad did what they always did in times like these, they prayed.

They prayed, and within hours, watched their loving God change a multi-colored, swollen, sick looking, stove pipe of a leg, back to what is was before. Healthy and whole.

And today he's a legend back at that little church camp in the hills of western Pennsylvania. His story has been told to hundreds of kids who visit the camp every year. A story about taking shortcuts. The power of prayer. And the lesson to be learned from it.

There are no shortcuts through Gruntsville. And even though you will be tempted to leave the path at the most difficult and dangerous places, you must not. You must resist the urge to take it. It only leads to futility.

You see, short cuts are really useless behaviors. They camouflage themselves as good business, smart thinking, and shrewd planning and deceive you into thinking you can gain a big advantage and beat all the others by doing so. But concealed beneath their veneer of quick and easy success lie the fangs of futility. Waiting to inject its deadly poison.

Someone once said, "there is no right way to do the wrong thing." And it's true.

There is no right way to wrong someone. No wrong path to travel in a right way.

But God knows how we try. How we try to buy, sell, extort, coerce, manipulate, deceive, con, bully, cheat, steal, lie, and slander, just to get ahead of all the others. To be first, on top, number one, the greatest and best.

Perhaps you know of someone who left the good path of life in an attempt to get to their thing before all the others. Putting themselves first, and concerned only about their needs and wants, as they pushed ahead in ignorance. Unaware of the snares and dangers that lay ahead.

I remember a bunch of talented athletes in high school, college, and the pro's, who took short cuts in their sports. And I can't remember one who escaped unharmed.

Some took short cuts in their conditioning. They didn't last.

Some took short cuts in their preparation. They made mistakes.

Some took short cuts by using drugs and alcohol. It's debilitating affects and the law eventually caught up to them.

You see, your treasure of reason and counsel of understanding were given to keep you from being smitten by the poisonous fangs of futility. From experiencing the awful, and painful affects short cuts can have in your life. They're your path to life. And are meant to guide you along and through the difficult circumstances of Gruntsville. And the book of Proverbs is full of promises for those who walk along straight paths. For those who do not stray from the way of wisdom.

So when you're tempted to take the easy way out of Gruntsville, to stray from the right way of doing things, just remember the fangs of futility that await you.

Determine right now to follow your council of understanding and treasure of reason. They will guide you along and direct your steps toward growth, opportunity and chance.

How do I know? Well, that nine year old kid who left the trail back there? It was me.

"Show me your ways, O Lord, teach me your paths; guide me in your truth and teach me, for you are God my Savior, and my hope is in you all day long." --Psalms 25:4-5. (NIV)

TIME OF POSSESSION

In Super Bowl XXV, our New York Giants offense controlled the football for well over two-thirds of the football game. It was perhaps the most critical factor in winning the game for us. We ran a ball-controlled offense, mixing hard hitting, effective rushing plays, with strategic passing plays, to wear down our opponent's defense, and eventually run out the clock.

In other words, what we did with the football, while we had it, between the start and finish of the game was significant. We didn't turn the ball over to the opposing team with fumbles, interceptions, or inept plays. We kept moving the football and first down markers progressively downfield, until we eventually scored a touchdown or field goal. It was an effective strategy. And it won each of us a Super Bowl ring.

Now that win didn't come easy for us. In fact, at one point, when I was sitting on the bench inhaling smelling salts after taking a vicious hit from Leon Seals, some would have thought the game was over. We were behind, and the Bills were trying to deliver a knock-out punch.

But we came back. Used the remaining time to our advantage. And won the game.

Now the funny thing is, Gruntsville is similar in many respects to that football game. There's a beginning and end to it. It starts the moment you engage your opposition, and ends when you have mastered its lessons. The quarterback is you. The coach is Wisdom. The gates are the first down markers. Your play book is your cabinet of imagination, treasure of reason, registry of conscience, and council chamber of thought. Your goal is growth, opportunity, and chance. Your arena is the village of Gruntsville, where the spectators are friends and foe alike, cheering and jeering you on. And the "Due Time" clock keeper is God Himself.

Now what's your strategy for winning? Your game plan for success? And have you factored in time of possession?

I hope so. Because if your Gruntsville experience goes anything like our Super Bowl game against the Buffalo Bills, you're going to need to use every precious second to your advantage, and eliminate turnovers.

You see, your Gruntsville will become a roller coaster ride of emotions as the game progresses. You will start the game with high optimism, certain of success. Probably hit the wall of doubt and pessimism when you get behind. Momentum will shift back and forth, and you might just find yourself struggling for consciousness on the bench after taking some vicious hits by your opponent. But if you don't quit, keep attacking, and control the football and the clock, your doubt will eventually turn to hope, and hope will renew your confidence and ultimately lead to success.

That's what happened to us. Don't be surprised if it happens to you.

Don't be surprised if things in Gruntsville happen that you didn't expect. Or if things don't happen that you did expect.

Don't be surprised if the hits you take disorient you or alter your perception of things. And don't be surprised by the difficulty in managing all this change and uncertainty. Be patient. Don't go into your hurry-up offense just yet. Be methodical. Plug along. Gain positive yardage with each play. Don't turn the ball over. Keep the momentum going. And please, don't worry about things you can't control or do. Focus on what you can control and do to maximize your time of possession.

I remember sitting at a small booth in a restaurant adjacent to the stage of the auditorium where Turner Network Television's live, nationally televised Saturday

Night Super Bowl XXVI Special was being presented in Minneapolis, Minnesota. I was there to make an appearance on stage with all of the quarterbacks from the NFL, and was enjoying a quiet moment with my brothers, and Dad, when one of America's best syndicated columnists, Andy Rooney, decided to join us. He told us the Super Bowl Committee asked him to write an article for the game program, offering him $3500 to do it. He responded to their offer by telling them, "what I have is $3500, but what I don't have is a hotel room and a ticket for the game."

Well, the Super Bowl Committee quickly got Mr. Rooney a hotel room and ticket to the game. But his response is what I often hear by so many in Gruntsville. So much time is wasted on thinking about what they don't have rather than focusing on what they do have. Of worrying about things they can't control rather than on things they can. And time is what all of us have, at this very moment, to use in a positive way, to advance, move the markers, and reach our goal of getting out of Gruntsville.

So it's important to take possession of your time. And to maximize its use while you still can.

Now I'm not promising it will win a Super Bowl ring for you. But I am promising you it will greatly affect the results of your performance depending on how you use it.

If you focus on what you have, and not on what you don't. If you hang in there when Gruntsville becomes an emotional roller coaster ride. If you stick to your game plan of controlling the ball and the clock. You will, in due time and due course, reap the rewards and satisfaction of managing the game clock of your life efficiently and effectively. Of having lived a full, purposeful and meaningful life.

But you have got to do it now. You must take possession of your time immediately. Understand its use. And then put it to work wisely as you climb your stairway to success.

Now, move on. You're burning daylight.

Redeem the time

THE PORT IN OPPORTUNITY

Halfway through the National Anthem he began to shake and tremble. Falling to one knee he tried to balance and steady himself as his inner world began to darken. A moment later, he was gone.

His teammates gathered around, as they watched their starting high school quarterback thrash around on the sideline. He skin began to turn a sickening blue as his body heaved up and down in a violent fit of rage. The countdown to death had begun.

Searching for someone to do something, his football coach frantically called for the trainer. Who struggled desperately against time, and cutting bars of gnashing, ivory teeth, to open the player's airway and save his life.

No one seemed to remember how long it took the trainer to open the boy's airway. To finally free the opening that was being held hostage by a slumbering tongue. And to hear the first sound of air that rushed into aching lungs. They only knew it had seemed too long.

Numb with fear, the boy's mother stepped from the crowd, and joined her unconscious son inside the ambulance that arrived moments later. And as the medics closed its doors, she silently wondered if the doors of his young life had just closed too.

The screaming siren of the ambulance haunted her along the way. It called up the ghost of death from the catacombs of her past. Reminding her of the day not long ago, when her sixteen year old brother Ronnie was pulled from the bottom of a river and taken away forever--the victim of a drowning accident.

And now, the parallels were shockingly similar. Another sixteen year old boy. Her flesh in blood. The ambulance. The siren. The Fear. And the name. For she had named this son after him.

But in that moment of horror, while she battled the demon of death, and the ghost of misery past, a still, small voice seemed to whisper hope in her ear. Reminding her of the port, the door that remained open to her God.

And so she prayed. Asking her Lord to breathe life into the heart, mind, and soul of her young son. To give him another opportunity at life.

And He did.

Hours later, her son awoke. His fatal fever was gone.

Medical tests and examinations revealed nothing. No spinal or viral meningitis as the doctors suggested. No brain damage. Not even a trace that anything had been wrong. (Of course his brothers and sisters said all along the doctors wouldn't find anything in his head.)

Well this kid turned out to be me. And you can bet I learned a very important lesson about ports. About open doors and opportunity. That we need to keep them open and unobstructed because the consequences can be disastrous.

You see, lungs need an open trachea. The heart needs open arteries. Families and partners need open communication. The quarterback needs an open receiver. And the running back needs an open field. Understanding needs an open mind. Love needs open arms. Giving needs an open hand. And opportunity needs an open door.

Unobstructed openings are critical to life, well being, and success. They're absolutely essential to functioning properly and performing effectively.

It's tragic the way we allow the trials and difficulties of Gruntsville to block the passages to our goals, and suffocate our dreams. The way we let the bumps and bruises of misfortune choke us from inhaling opportunity, growth, and chance.

But when it does, there is help available. And the God of Gruntsville is the trainer that will do it for you. He will free whatever's blocking your way and open the port of future opportunities if you just keep your airway to Him open. He's there to help you reignite your imagination, rekindle your conscience, refocus your thoughts, and restore your reason. There to help pull you up and through the suffocating streets of Gruntsville, step after step, one lesson at a time.

Jeff and I both remember the suffocating streets of Gruntsville. The numbing sensation that slowly overcame us as our problems and difficulties strangled our hope. But just when everything seemed hopeless, a still, small voice reminded us of the opening we had to the gates of heaven. And just like mom, we prayed. Not for fame and fortune. But for God to rebuild, renew, and restore us. To keep us from succumbing to the noxious fumes of Gruntsville while we journeyed through, listening, and learning from Him as we went.

So keep your airways and pathways open and unobstructed while you trudge along the streets of Gruntsville. Particularly your airway to the gates of heaven. When you feel the choking affects of unexpected disaster, pray. Pray and ask for renewed understanding and hope. Don't wait. Don't pray as a last resort. Do it now, before time and circumstance consume the remaining air you have.

Inhale this lesson for a few moments. Let it saturate your lungs. Give thanks to God for its life giving force. And then move on. You have much more to learn.

"Be careful, then, how you live--not as unwise but as wise, making the most of every opportunity, because the days are evil"

Ephesians 5:16

THE PHD ADVANTAGE

Turn left off old route 601, just beyond its intersection with the 219 bypass, and you'll see the street marker that says "Hostetler Road", "Home of Jeff Hostetler." It was placed there by township officials in honor of Jeff's outstanding Super Bowl XXV performance and win over the Buffalo Bills.

And depending on how you look at it, the sign marks the beginning and end of the dirt lane which leads to and from our Pennsylvania homestead. A 130 acre poultry and dairy farm nestled in the hills of Somerset County.

Now we walked this long dirt journey every weekday to catch the school bus. And we walked it regardless of the weather. Rain or shine. Snow or sleet. We walked. Sometimes repeating it twice a day if we had evening practice or away games to play.

Sometimes we complained. Sometimes we argued for a better, easier means of transportation. But with a farm, seven kids, and all its demands, mom and dad didn't have the time to drive us out the lane and sit with us until the bus came. Did it hurt us? Was it unfair to make us walk that distance everyday to school, regardless of the weather, when all the other kids had it easier and more convenient that we did? Not in the least. But we wouldn't have said that then.

You see, that street marker at the end of the lane could have said, "Hostetler Road, Home of the poor, hungry, and driven.

Poor, as in poor in spirit. In other words we were taught to walk through life with a humble dependence on God rather than on personal power, talents, or other resources. Not that we had much anyway.

Hungry, as in hungry to learn. That is, we had a teachable appetite. An openness and willingness to learn the lessons of life.

And driven, as in driven to apply. We had a passion to grow. To put into practice the lessons we were being taught on the farm.

In short, this was our PHD advantage. Our degree path to success, although at first it looked to us like a disadvantage. But things are not always as they seem.

You see, that simple dirt lane led to a simple life on a simple place. Nothing pretentious or showy about it. Just plain and simple. Sort of like Penn State's uniforms.

We were non-conformists too, just like Paterno. He didn't allow the rest of the world to squeeze him or his team into their mold. Although at times we sort of wish he had. When all the other football teams were sporting flashy new uniforms, we stayed with the plain Jane look. When all the other teams seemed to be cutting deals and corners in their attempts to recruit the best and brightest, Paterno cut straight to the point. His way was going to be simple and straight forward. Work hard. Stay humble. Learn from him and his coaches, and apply it with everything you got, every practice. If you did what he said, Saturday's game would take care of itself.

Mom and dad were the same way. Their way was straight forward, honest, and simple. Work hard. Stay humble. Learn from them and God, apply it with everything you got, everyday, and your future would take care of itself.

They didn't give into what we wanted. Rather, they gave us what we needed. And that was a wiry work ethic, a forceful focus, an engaging environment, a powerful purpose, a divine determination, a competitive core, an incredible imagination, a running spring of resourcefulness, and a passion to persevere.

Somehow they knew that giving us too much would be giving us too little. They knew a good work ethic, humble heart, and teachable spirit would be hard to develop in us if our bellies were full of self-indulgence, comfort and ease.

They knew the dangers of saturating the heart and mind with empty entertainment and meaningless, mindless Madison Avenue pursuits. And so they weaned us on the essentials. The basics. Their PHD curriculum of success.

You see, we didn't have VCR's, CD players or personal computer games in our home competing for our time. And we didn't wear the latest fashions, live in the classiest neighborhood, or drive the most expensive cars. Not that these things are inherently bad mind you. But they were trivial pursuits compared to what mattered.

We hardly ever ate out or received much if any allowance. Rarely took vacations or days off from our chores, even when we were sick. We worked seven days a week, including holidays, went to church, and took Sunday afternoon naps as mini-vacations.

We used coat hangers for rims to play basketball. Used tattered wiffle balls to shoot with, gravel and dirt to play on, and the side of the chicken house for a backboard. You see, we didn't have breakaway rims, macadamed surfaces to play on, or "Air Jordans" to play in. And when the weather got bad, we built our own indoor sports coliseum inside the metal grain bin, stringing up a few lights in order to play at night after chores. And even though the protruding nuts and bolts tore up our knuckles and skinned our shoulders on our driving lay-ups, we healed. But you know what? We got better. We improved, in spite of our lack of resources.

Yes, on the outside it didn't look like we had much. But if you think we sat around feeling sorry for ourselves, you're mistaken. We didn't have time for that. Besides, mom and dad wouldn't allow it. They understood the principle, "necessity breeds invention." So they engaged us with chores needing done, problems to solve, and difficulties to fix. And it led to growth. The result of an enterprising mix of imagination, invention, creation, and engineering.

Now the point of all this is simple. Gruntsville is like life on a farm, and it's a great lesson in problem solving and character building. But its trials and tribulations will have you sitting in the corner, sucking your thumb, and feeling sorry for yourself if your not careful. You will think you have not been given all the advantages in life that others have. You will look at your situation, compare it with others, and figure that life isn't fair. You'll feel deprived, overworked, and isolated. And this can lead to self-indulgence, materialism, and a belly full of stuff that will weigh you down, and prevent you from succeeding.

It takes the inner steel of self-discipline, self-control, and self-denial to stay humble, hungry, and on purpose. It's the structure of success. A matter that matters. And it's up to you to allow the iron furnaces of Gruntsville to forge this inner steel in you by smelting away the self-indulgent excesses in your life.

So when you begin to feel sorry for yourself in Gruntsville, and your trials and tribulations have you sitting in the corner, sucking your thumb, just remember this lesson. When you think you have not been given the kinds of advantages in life that others have, and figure life just isn't fair when you look around and compare your situation to others. Just turn your poor, hungry, and driven appetite into a PHD degree to success. Don't get suckered into thinking everything you want is good for you. It's not. In fact, getting too much may be getting too little. Too little of what you really need to succeed.

Poor, hungry and driven. Let this lesson soak in for a moment. Turn the pages of its truth over and over in your mind until it becomes a part of you. Tread it out in your daily walk down the lane of life. And you'll eventually have your own sign of success too, posted at the end of your life lane.

BLOOD DRILL

It was "Bloody Tuesday."

Compared to any other day of the week, this was the worst. Particularly if we had lost the football game the Saturday before.

You see, "Bloody Tuesday" was the day our linebacking corps did some smash mouth, face busting, toe to toe hitting and tackling. It was a day for high octane explosions as we propelled ourselves into one another, kamikaze style.

It was a day for getting better. For sharpening our skills. And our appetite for perfection. Because that's what the coaches wanted, and demanded, perfection. No mistakes. No defects. Just flawless, unsurpassed excellence.

Our linebacking coach, Jerry Sandusky, conducted a drill on these particular Tuesdays to perfect his players. And appropriately enough, it was called "Blood Drill."

"Blood Drill" was a three on one contest. That's right, three on one. Coach Sandusky would stand behind the single player and direct the other three facing him to attack on command. That single linebacker, standing one step from the others, would have to "read" each attackers approach in an instant, step up, deliver a counter strike, and then gather and realign himself as quickly as possible to meet the next attacker, and so on. It was a rapid fire drill. And it tested strength, leverage, quickness, balance, agility, perception, ability to adjust, and particularly toughness.

All of these skills are highly valued and necessary to acquire and develop in life as well as in football. And they need to be tested to determine their quality. Therefore you must develop a planned training program to do it. Because if you don't, someone else will. That's what coaches, parents, and employers are for.

You see, they know you need strength of heart, mind, body and soul to carry out your duties and responsibilities.

They know you need leverage, the power to influence or dominate. The skill or ability to lift great problems by using your mind and will as a lever and fulcrum.

They know you will need to think fast, prepare promptly, react speedily and respond quickly when situations demand it.

They know you need mental and emotional steadiness in your work. Poise under pressure to keep you from jumping off sides by the "hard counts" of life.

They know you need agility, the ability to adjust, to stay on your feet while everything or everyone else around you changes directions.

They know you need discernment, insight, and a keen awareness of what's going on around you so you can respond appropriately.

And they know you need toughness to get you through. We call it inner steel. It's the kind of stuff that is flexible but not brittle. An ability to undergo great strain. The capacity to stand hard work and hardship, marked by a firm uncompromising determination.

This is the stuff Jerry wanted to develop in us. And blood drill was his way of bringing it about.

In fact, blood drill was a secret right of passage for Penn State linebackers. You see it required using the forehead of the helmet with such force and in such a way that it would often tear the flesh right above the bridge of the nose if you performed it correctly. And when hot blood dripped down your face, you became a blood brother, a lifetime card carrying member of the Penn State linebacking corps.

I remember my first "Blood Drill." It was like the Roman days, when for sport, the emperor would throw the Christians into the arena with the lions. I barely survived, and didn't want to do it again. I suffered a slight concussion, whip lash, and cuts and bruises on my arms. But it wasn't until a year later that Jerry danced around me like an Indian on the warpath, hoop'n and holler'n because I did the drill right. And I guess I had. I was bleeding from the bridge of my nose.

The same drill and deal applied to everyone. Keep drilling and drilling until you perfect the skill, and master the deal. Excellence requires repetition, and someone or something to sharpen your skills. "Bloody Tuesday", and "Blood Drill" provided both.

And you know what? Gruntsville does too. It provides a practice field, a coach, and challenging forces to sharpen the skills you need to succeed.

You will have your "Bloody Tuesdays" and "Blood Drills" in Gruntsville. Days when you will go up against seemingly insurmountable forces. Days when you will feel like you have just been thrown into a lions den.

When you do, remember the purpose of these days and this drill. It's purpose is to sharpen you. To perfect your skills. And to keep you accountable. Stuff you need to succeed.

There's an old Proverb that says, "As iron sharpens iron, so one man sharpens another." It means all of us need someone in our lives who will look us in the eye and challenge our thoughts, intentions, motives, and behavior. Someone who will ask the tough questions. Check our choices, and help decipher our decisions. Someone closer than a brother, who will demonstrate "tough love" rather than let us alone to wallow in self-pity and despair.

Coach Sandusky demonstrated this kind of tough love. So did my Mom and Dad. And my brother Doug. They challenged me. They reprimanded me. They encouraged me to get better. To perfect my attitude, skills, and behavior.

At times I thought they were cruel, unkind, and uncaring. But they could sense when I needed a kick in the butt, and when I needed an encouraging word.

When I needed discipline, and when I needed devotion. When I needed practice, and when I needed rest. When I needed pushed, and when I needed support.

All of us need a "Bloody Tuesday" and a "Blood Drill" now and then, to keep us accountable, and to sharpen our skills. Someone to practice against, and someone to coach us through it.

Who do you have to keep you accountable?

Who do you have to coach you through these kinds of trying, difficult days and drills?

Perhaps it's a parent, coach, teacher, sibling, pastor, wife, husband, employer, counselor, or close friend. If you do have someone like this, someone who is willing to challenge, push, demand, question, pry, stimulate, excite, and test you, count yourself fortunate. Listen to them. Learn from them. And don't get angry at them when they don't let you off easy, or give in to your lame excuses for not getting better. They can help you.

And if you don't have someone, look around. Find someone you look up to. Someone who has successfully gone through the gates of Gruntsville. And ask them to mentor you through your bloody Tuesdays and blood drills of your life.

Remember too, you can always call for help from the One who knows and understands what it means to bleed for the sake of others. The bloody Tuesdays and blood drills of life are His way of making us better and more useful for sacrificial service to our team of humanity. His Proverb is meant for you. So fasten it down in your mind. Secure it to your heart. And anchor it to your soul. As iron sharpens iron, It will eventually help you develop the things you need to succeed in Gruntsville.

DANDELIONS OF DEVOTION

It was his last act of devotion.

With tears in his eyes, and a broken heart, he handed me a small clump of dandelions to place in her hands.

As a toddler, he would frequently go out into the fields and pick them for her with his chubby, grubby little paws. Greatly anticipating the sunny smile, and warm embrace that would follow. And then he would watch as she carefully placed them in a vase for all the world to see how much he loved her.

But today, her hands no longer moved. Neither could they reach out or accept the gift he was giving. Mom was gone.

Twenty-nine years after giving birth to a future Super Bowl hero, Mom died. Leaving behind the memory of hands that had nurtured, cared for, and lovingly held--him.

No longer would she be there to confide in. To offer tips and suggestions on how to raise and discipline his kids. Or how to maximize marriage and resolve conflict.

No more phone calls of counsel. No more cards to inspire. Bible verses to memorize. Books to read. Or tapes to listen to.

No more words of praise. Or notes of encouragement in the mail. No more prayers of faith that seemed to move mountains. No more soprano solos that shook the heavens.

Her eyes, her hands, her feet, her voice, slumbered in silent stillness as the coffin closed in a final wave of goodbye to her son standing by. Watching as it entombed his first love and the small clump of flowers that would forever symbolize his undying, unyielding, love and affection for her. His dandelions of devotion.

How does a heart learn devotion? How can it keep on beating when the sting of death bludgeons it with sorrow? And how is it today, that devotion is so often taken for granted? Allowed to lie fallow after childhood. Only to reawaken when it is shook by emergency and circumstance.

It is good to remember childhood devotion. To recall our meager attempts at expressing a flowering heart. God knew how we felt as a child. And so He placed within our reach, and within our grasp, flowering fields of dandelions to gather and give to our first loves.

And it's the same today. God has placed within our reach, and within our grasp, flowering fields of dandelions-- words, expressions, embraces-- to gather and give to those we love and cherish.

But we must not allow it to lie idle during the growing seasons of life. We must reawaken childhood devotion, and practice it daily. Before the growing season is over, and it's too late.

So today, while you still can. Take a moment to devote yourself to reawakening the ardent love and affection you once held for your parents, spouse, and children. Center your attention on them for a moment. Set aside a special time to embrace them with a gentle hug, a caring card, an affectionate note, or a word of praise and love.

And while you do, notice their response. Listen to their voice. Look into their eyes. Touch their hands. Remember the embrace. And savor the moment. Because the brevity of life will take them from you all too soon.

Dandelions of devotion. You might not see them at first, but Gruntsville is full of them. And they are there to remind you of the importance and significance of devotion. To remind you that your team, family, or company needs your dedicated support and service to accomplish their mission.

You see, dedication means to set apart for some purpose and especially a sacred or serious purpose. And since it implies self-sacrificing devotion, the question becomes, to whom or to what have you dedicated your life to?

In our family we were taught to be devoted to one another. And for the most part we were. Although we fought a lot among ourselves, there was no questioning our devotion, especially when somebody outside our family picked a fight with one of us. Every single one would come charging to the rescue when that ever happened. And it was great to feel its fervor.

And of course it was the same on the gridiron. One moment we could be arguing and fighting among ourselves during a game, and the next moment defending each other from our opponents like a raging grizzly bear.

This is why there is such a thing as devotion. It's there to bond people together. Devotion builds trust and faith in one another. And it leads to great things, especially when one is willing to lay down everything he has, even his life for the sake or benefit of a person, idea or cause. Just think of the devotion, the dedicated self-sacrificing service demonstrated by our men and women of uniform. And the numbers who died, who paid the ultimate sacrifice for our freedoms.

So as you journey through Gruntsville, pick some dandelions like my brother Jeff used to do and give them to someone in remembrance of their inspired devotion. And make sure to keep one for yourself as a reminder for what you have been set apart to do. You have a mission to accomplish, a sacred purpose to fulfill. Therefore dedicate yourself to it. Serve with honor. Serve with dignity. And give yourself away in an act of undying, unyielding devotion.

Believe me, you won't be forgotten.

"Be devoted to one another in brotherly love. Honor one another above yourselves. Never be lacking in zeal, but keep your spiritual fervor, serving the Lord."
--Romans 12:10-11 (NIV)

INJURIES OF INJUSTICE

Lightning struck!

Back-pedaling to cover a pass, I planted my foot on the hard, unyielding astroturf. Suddenly, a sharp searing pain bolted through my knee. I hobbled to the sideline like a crippled deer, and collapsed on the bench in excruciating pain.

No matter what I tried, I just couldn't get my knee to respond to the messages my brain was sending it. Our team doctor went quickly to work assessing the damage.

But the look in his eyes told me all I had to know. It was bad. And after putting my knee through a series of painful maneuvers and tests, his diagnosis hit me like a bolt of lightning. Torn cartilage and ligaments, possibly the anterior cruciate. I was shocked.

I sat there in disbelief, riveted to the bench with the grip of fear. This was the kind of injury that ends football careers. How could this have happened to me? I was the captain of our team, a preseason All American and according to Joe Paterno, his next Jack Ham (Pittsburgh Steelers All Pro Linebacker and former Penn State All-American). I was trying hard to be positive, but my worst nightmare had just occurred. Considered high draft potential in the National Football league at the beginning of the season, my stock immediately fell. After all, who's going to draft damaged goods. And so I painfully watched my dream of becoming a star in the N.F.L. melt away, just like the ice pack on my injured knee, as I sat there all alone in the locker room of Vet stadium.

We went on to win the game against Temple that day, but I felt I was the loser. I had become a statistic. Another unlucky winner in Mother Nature's cruel game of chance. Another victim of big time college football. And though the pain in my knee would eventually subside, the pain in my heart wouldn't .

It was painful watching someone else take my place. Once considered the "mainstay" of our defense, I was now a useless casualty. A broken piece of machinery that had to be replaced. That's how I felt. It's the way things were. I realized for the very first time how expendable I was. That I was a piece of equipment in a football machine that didn't have time for breakdowns. Just a replaceable part. I guess it's the way it has to be at this level of competition.

You see, injuries are frustrating, painful and unjust. Frustrating because they aren't expected and mess up plans. Painful because they're shocking, producing physical, and emotional trauma. And unjust because they appear to strike randomly without just cause or due process.

And although I eventually made a come back from my injury, I was never quite the same. Not quite as quick, as fast or as agile as I once was. Even though I was later drafted by the Los Angeles Rams.

But if you think I joined shock victims anonymous to sit around feeling sorry for myself because of this misfortunate injury, think again. I discovered God has a way of turning injuries of injustice into something good if you just let Him.

There's a verse I remember in a song titled, "Heads or Tails", that says; "Sometimes we try to blaze our own trail, we make our plans in every detail, it's easy to think that we're in control but God only knows where your life will go".

I discovered there's no way to control things like injuries. I had worked hard at doing everything I could to prevent them, but this was one thing I couldn't control. And as much as I tried to blaze my own trail on my way to the NFL frontier I couldn't control the random acts of injustice that would strike me along the way. I could plan, prepare, and persevere to make it a successful journey, but there was no way I could control all the outside, circumstantial forces and factors that would hit me.

But there was one thing I could control, and I know you've heard this over and over again, but it's true. I could control my response. I had the capacity to react favorably, the ability to reply positively, responsibly, and religiously. Everyone has this. All of us have been given the ability to turn tragedy into triumphs if we just let God have our ashes when lightning strikes.

You see many equate the term victim with weakness. In other words, victims are people who lack strength or are unable to sustain or resist much weight, pressure, or strain. That they are deficient, feeble, ineffective and impotent, and somehow responsible for their circumstances. Well, this may be bad news to some, but to others its good news, because the God of justice comes down clearly on the side of victim's rights. He's the greatest advocate a victim can have. And you can be sure He can take you from ashes to glory in a very short time.

In the Bible it says that "God chose the weak things of the world to shame the strong." And that "He chose the lowly things of this world and the despised things--and the things that are not--to nullify the things that are, so that no one may boast before him." In addition, God went on to assure one of His self-confessed weakest missionaries that "My grace is sufficient for you, for my power is made perfect in weakness."

The point is simple. At the moments of our greatest weakness, God shows and proves Himself strong. Strong enough to bring us up from the ashes of despair. But we must acknowledge and call upon Him for help. That's our choice. And that can and should be our response when lightning strikes.

So when injuries of injustice strike you down like a bolt of lightning during the thunderstorms of Gruntsville, and they will, consider your response because you're probably going to need resuscitation. You will need revived when they strike because they will pack enough power in their punch to light a small city, capable of blowing the rivets out of your plans, stopping the beating passions of your heart, jolting the justice in your journey, and melting the mission in your pocket of change.

If and when it does, turn your ashes over to the Lord. Let Him become your victim's rights advocate. Let him turn your weakness into strength. Let him revive, renew, restore and rivet in you the kinds of attitudes, skills and values that will bring glory to His creation.

If you do, count on Him to rivet your plans with purpose, redirect your journey, jump start the moral flat liner in your heart, and coin new currency to exchange for a meaningful life.

No, you don't have to remain in sackcloth and ashes in Gruntsville. Learn this lesson, apply its truth and watch God raise you from ashes to glory.

Here are a few suggestions when injuries of injustice strike you:

1. Realize God is still in control. In spite of everything understand that if you are God's, He's still working out His plans for your life. You might have to change YOUR travel plans as the apostle Paul did in 2nd Corinthians, but God has placed His seal of ownership upon you, guaranteeing your final destination. You can be assured He is faithful in all of this.

2. Realize you are not alone. Although you will FEEL isolated and useless, God promised to be with you always and everywhere.

3. Understand that your VALUE to God is not based upon your success as an athlete, parent, student, employee, or

entrepreneur. His desire is for us to become more like Him as we struggle through Gruntsville.

4. Work hard at overcoming your injury of injustice. Some injuries of injustice are career ending, others are not. Get proper assistance and counsel. Rehabilitating, or retooling oneself for success is one of the toughest challenges any of us will face. You must determine to work hard, even though it may be painful and take a lot of time.

5. Be Patient. Relax and rest in God's grace. Injuries of injustice slow us down.. So use this time to read and study God's word which will encourage your heart.

6. Don't lose Heart. Losing heart is destructive.. Watch over your heart with all diligence. Keep it filled with the knowledge of His will by reading good books, listening to good things and spending time with successful people.

7. Find a Friend for Support. Proverbs 27:17 says "As iron sharpens iron, so one man sharpens another". Don't let yourself crawl away to a cave somewhere to wallow in self pity. A good friend will help you keep perspective and challenge you to work hard at overcoming your injury of injustice.
8. Stay in touch with key members of your team, organization or family. They still need your leadership and encouragement even though you may not feel like giving it.

9. Memorize Galatians 6:9. Remember that in "Due Time" you will reap a reward for doing good throughout your struggle. Learn to laugh. Keep a sense of humor, it will be healing to your bones.

10. Draw upon the support of your family and church. They will pray for you and intercede to God on your behalf. There's no place like home and family to mend broken limbs as well as broken hearts and dreams.

11. Read. Read. And read. Books are benevolent benefactors, master mentors, so devour them. Consume them. Possess them and they will possess you. Mrs. Charles E. Cowman once said, "The more we read the more we believe, the more we believe the more we hope, the more we hope the more we pray, the more we pray the more we love, the more we love the more we labor.

Remember, don't play the "If Only" game. That is, if only I would have stretched better, or if only I had worked a little harder, or if only I wouldn't have gotten hurt, I could have been........ This stuff is very destructive and it won't help. Keep your mind fixed on the things that will give you a hope and a future.

God has a way of recycling damaged goods and turning tragedies into opportunities. Look at the story of Joseph who was sold by his brothers into slavery in Egypt. In due time Joseph discovered God's purpose. He told his brothers they meant it for evil but God turned it into good. God will do the same for you. He did for me.

Just remember, *the worst thing that ever happens to you, might be the best thing that ever happens to you, if you don't let it get the best of you."*

A GAME OF TOUCH

I recently heard a former National Football League coach say of a certain NFL quarterback that "He has such a strong arm, he could throw a football through a car wash without getting it wet." Don't you just love prime time television hype?

Now there are certainly a few NFL trigger men who possess enough fire power in their high caliber, six-million dollar (or more) "guns" to send the best of receivers to the emergency room with third degree powder burns on their hands. But high powered deliveries aren't always good, nor wise to use, particularly in Gruntsville.

You see, sometimes a quarterback will encounter special passing situations that require him to put some "touch" on the ball--to lower the powder charge and change the trajectory in order to loft a ball softly over a defender, or to ensure that the receiver catches it. And the amount of "touch" required by the quarterback, usually depends on the "hands" of the receiver, and the distance and obstacles that lie between them.

Unfortunately, for some quarterbacks, this is a difficult thing to learn. And if they don't learn it, they won't succeed at the level they could.

Now some of you are not succeeding at the level you could because of this very thing. You have not developed the concept of "touch" in your communication and interpersonal relationships. Nor have you taken the time to consider its value. It seems some of you would rather touch off high octane explosions with high powered deliveries than take the time, energy or effort to lower your caliber and change your trajectory in order to throw a more a receptive pass.

In Gruntsville, both of us have learned that rifling high powered remarks and advice to others is not always good, nor wise. We're both trying to develop a more sensitive touch in our communication and interpersonal skills. The kind of touch and trajectory that will ensure a reception by our colleagues, families and business associates--not sting 'em and blister 'em to kingdom come.

No, if you want to advance the ball, maintain momentum, and help your team win, you gotta put some touch on the ball. And that's exactly what this lesson in Gruntsville is all about.

Do you feel like you're not connecting with your wife? Husband? Kids? Or business associates? Like you're not getting through? Or like everything you say and do is just bouncing off unreceptive hearts and ears?

Well, maybe you need to lower the caliber, and change the trajectory of your delivery. Maybe you need to learn to put some touch on the ball. And that may mean more than just softening, or rephrasing your words. It may actually mean sending your message in a more sensitive way, using a hug, embrace, kiss, or two hand touch to ensure reception.

This is a skill that can be developed. But you must begin to monitor your passes and the reception styles of your receivers. Find out what obstacles may be keeping their hands and hearts closed to you, rather than open. Get some feedback from them. What kind of hands do they have? In other words how receptive are they to different methods of communication? Do they prefer a "cut to the chase" delivery, or a more personal, indirect means of communication?

Whatever the response, and we hope it is a response and not a reaction, make whatever half-time adjustments you need in order to help them win. In doing so, you will help yourself in the process. Remember, it takes touch to play this game effectively.

"Saul also went to his home in Gibeah, accompanied by valiant men whose hearts God had touched.
I Samuel 10:26 (NIV)

WHERE HAVE YOU GONE TOM AND BURT?

With iron will and rugged determination they fixed their gaze on the task before them, sensitive to the hand upon their reins and the voice directing their steps.

Their names? Tom and Burt. Sixteen hundred pounds of bridled beauty. A team of workhorses wed to a simple task of carving out a living in the Pennsylvania countryside for a Mennonite family.

And the hands upon their reins? They belonged to a young lad called "Jr." --our Dad.

Oh, what a sight it was as Dad recalled his boyhood days with Tom & Burt, giving a history lesson to his grandchildren who were huddled around the kitchen table in the old farmhouse.

It was to be our last holiday celebration together on a homestead built at the turn of the century by our great grandfather Joseph. Things had changed. It was time to sell. Time to move on.

But most of all it was time to remember. It was time to capture the past before it passed us. A time to reflect on generations of experiences that had somehow, some way, woven themselves into the character of our own families.

Sure, Tom and Burt are gone. So is the old barn that was destroyed by fire years back. Gone are the days of slopping hogs, milking cows, hauling manure, bailing hay and gathering eggs.

Gone are the days of picking peas, canning corn, selling milk and delivering eggs. So are the days of walking the dirt lane, making tunnels in the hay mow, and doing donuts in the fields with the old Ford truck.

Watching dad's face, as he spoke of days gone by, was like watching the sun set beyond the hills, when it would cast a golden glow upon fields. We remember those fields well.

We remember their embrace, and how they charmed us as we walked and worked together, hand in hand, planting their seeds and cultivating their bounty. They put on a variety show of sorts for us as we gazed upon their colored beauty, and listened to their wind songs of praise from our perch on top of the hay mow just inside the giant open barn doors. It was like going to the movies.

But a somber silence has settled over those fields since the auction last fall. All is gone.

Or is it?

Although the landscape has changed, the memories remain. Memories of a distant time and a different place. Tom and Burt are symbolic of that time and of that place. A time and place that embraced and passed on rock solid, time-tested, enduring values. Values like simplicity, a solid work ethic, allegiance to duty, loyalty, fear of God, respect for authority, teamwork, self-restraint, perseverance and yes, character.

Tom and Burt. Those two workhorses possess a magical history that comes to life every time we remember. A history that helps us understand who we are, where we are, and why we are where we are.

You see, in those horses, and the fields they worked, past becomes present and history becomes future because they live in us. We carry their memories with us into the future. And build our futures from the ashes of their past. That's why Tom and Burt may be gone, but they're not forgotten. They live on, because they live in us.

Where have you gone Tom and Burt?

You have passed into the hearts and memory banks of your master's bloodline. Your story, and the symbolism it represents, along with many others, will be told and passed on to generations beyond ours, generations yet to come.

No, all is not gone, nor forgotten. And you must remember this when Gruntsville changes the landscape of your life. When the adversity of Gruntsville auctions off your prized possessions. When its fields of frustration produce nothing but fallow sorrow in your soul.

When change comes, and it will. You must move on. But you also must remember. You must remember that moving on doesn't mean all is gone. No way. What it does mean is you must build a new future from the ashes of your past, just like our Dad did when our barn burned down. It means planting new seeds of opportunity from the kernels of the past. And when you do this, it will inspire your heart, increase your faith, strengthen your resolve, cultivate your character and quicken your hope--for years and generations to come. Remember.

For the Psalmist writes, "Let this be written for a future generation, that a people not yet created may praise the Lord."

RING OF HONOR

It wasn't before millions of fans on television. Or embellished with pomp and circumstance.

There was no Star Spangled Banner. No wreath. No gold medal given.

It was a simple ceremony. Held at our dinner table. Recognizing the honor one of the kids had brought to our family.

Perhaps it was a small deed in the eyes of the world, and the eyes of this child, but in the eyes of her father, it was monumental. And it was not going to go unnoticed. Unrecognized. Or unrewarded.

With butter knife laying prostrate on his outstretched hand, Dad arose, gently dubbing the honor of knighthood upon the crown, of his now slightly embarrassed daughter, recognizing the public esteem and respect she had brought to their homeland.

And with words that would never adequately describe the fullness of her deed, or her father's heart, he christened her with a profession of affirmation.

It took only a moment. Only a few short seconds. But it was a moment in time that would be treasured for years to come.

Where has honor gone?

Where has the value of a good name, public esteem, reputation, chastity, purity, integrity, and respect gone?

It seems to have been put to rest somehow. Lying dormant beneath the skin and bones of empty people. People too busy, too hurried, and perhaps too consumed with things other than honor.

Honoring a father and a mother suggests the idea of taking parents seriously. Of giving importance in one's life, and paying attention to their place in our lives. And as a principle for effective living in the family, it has a universal quality that strengthens family relationships.

It's been said that, marriage should be honored by all. It is based upon a covenant relationship, and symbolized with a ring. A ring of honor that implies infinite purity, fidelity, chastity, respect, and integrity in its commitment.

But how can a child honor parents who don't honor one another? How can children attain the honor of a good name if it is being shamed by dishonorable acts? And how can children experience the delightful benefits of a chaste lifestyle if it is being polluted by disgusting things?

No, honor cannot be experienced, felt, or achieved, unless, and until, it is valued. And the place to demonstrate its value, is at home, in the family.

It begins with Dad honoring his God by acknowledging Him as author and giver of such magnificent things. This act, then establishes a framework and a model, for honoring one another in the home. And it is crucial if we are to turn the tide of turbulent times in our homeland. If we are to experience honor in the boardrooms, classrooms, bedrooms, and family rooms of America while we still have a thread of it left.

So as you sit down at the vanishing "dinner table" with your family tonight, pause for a moment, and reflect on the ring of honor you wear on your hand. Does it symbolize the honor you vowed to bestow on your spouse? Does it reflect the commitment you made to your family? Does it remind you of the God above who created you for honorable things?

I hope it does.

And I hope you don't despair if it doesn't.

It's never too late to begin the adventure of living honorably. As you stop at this gate in Gruntsville to consider its value, allow God to figuratively slip His ring of honor on your finger. It will remind you of the covenant relationship He has established with you. It will remind you of His integrity. It will remind you of the good things He wants you to experience and build into your life. The glorious virtues of purity, fidelity, chastity, respect and integrity. God knows how we need these things in our lives.

So let God crown your life with His honor. Saturate your mind and spirit with its virtue. Tread it out in your daily walk. Practice the precepts that develop it. Train yourself to become it. And continue to live honorably in your climb toward success. Your children and colleagues will probably notice the difference, particularly if you begin using the butter knife like King Arthur.

"..You are not your own; you were bought at a price.
Therefore honor God with your body."

I Corinthians 6:20-21

They're kind of funny looking. Just skin and guts. No real structure to them. Nothing to hold them up or support them. So they just sit and sag in a pathetic looking manner.

They're more vulnerable and susceptible to injury than the normal ones.

Breaking and bleeding easier than the rest, because they are unable to defend themselves from the nicks, cuts and pressures of life.

Some would say they're worthless. Good for nothing but the garbage heap.

But not us. We found them to be unique, and very useful, in spite of their limitations and diminished value. Especially the little ones. Because they bounced.

We called them "Rubber Eggs." Eggs without a shell. And they usually came from a mother hen lacking the right kind and amount of nutrients in her system.

We'd find at least a couple of them each day as we worked our way up and down the long concrete isles of the chicken house gathering eggs. It was our daily ritual on the farm. A menial task that required a nimble, flexible and sensitive touch, along with patience, persistence, and practice to prevent us from cracking or dropping them on the floor.

We loved finding these little yoked cush balls. And would carefully stow them away on our egg carts until we met up with our other two brothers who were also collecting eggs, but on opposite sides of the long isles of cages we were working.

You see, we loved competing against each other to see who the fastest egg gatherers were, and would do anything to slow each other down. So armed with a good supply of rubber eggs, and without any warning, we would whip them across the isles hoping to splatter them between the eyes.

And of course, we always had to plan for a quick escape in case they had their own supply too. And when they did, the hunter would become the hunted, leaving nothing but a wake of dust and chicken feathers flying from the ensuing chase that followed.

You see, we used rubber eggs to throw at each other because they were expendable. They had diminished value because they weren't developed properly. They didn't have the structure an egg was supposed to have and so their capacity as a marketable and attractive food item dropped in proportion to their under-development. And since they weren't developed properly they were used for something other than their intended purpose. So we used them for target practice against one another. In fact, throwing them around probably helped develop our passing, shooting and throwing skills in sports.

Now, looking back, those rubber eggs remind us of what life would be like without structure. What it would be like to grow up without the right framework, necessary construction, or adequate support everyone needs to succeed. Without structure, your capacity is crippled, your potential paralyzed, your purpose periled and your future jeopardized. Like a rubber egg you would just sit and sag, unable to protect or preserve your potential and purpose, or defend yourself for that matter, from the pecking problems of Gruntsville.

You know, in many ways, the story of the chicken and the egg is the story of Gruntsville. Not in which came first, but in the matter of structure. In other words, the matter of matter.

You see, matter in one sense is the substance of which a physical object is composed. It's something that occupies space and has weight and has a particular form and function.

In another sense, matter is a subject of interest or concern. It's something to be dealt with, as in a condition affecting a person or thing unfavorably.

Well, Gruntsville is a matter of interest to all of us because it is a condition affecting us unfavorably. And because it's an important concern, it matters. And what matters in Gruntsville is the substance of which you are composed. Because your composition will determine your future use. That is, your structure will determine your form and function. Whether you fulfill your potential, or just sit and sag like a rubber egg, occupying space, not pulling your weight.

And just as rubber eggs come from a hen lacking the right amount and kind of nutrients, so will the nutrients you consume during your incubation period in Gruntsville determine the nature and strength of your exiting framework. This is a fact. It is true. It is the way things are and in accord with how things are constructed. And just as architectural engineers plan, design and help build things according to methods, procedures and principles that are true, so too must you build the structure of your life on this truth.

Now think about this for a moment, and then correlate it to the Maroon Platoon Cocoon and "Due Time" dimension illustrations we shared with you. In many ways the maroon platoon symbolizes a bunch of underdeveloped rubber eggs. Like the 'Dirty Dozen" they were a company of athletes with diminished capacities, capabilities, and marketable team value, so they became expendable, used as practice dummies and for target practice by the varsity team. Their challenge, while stuck inside the womb of their cocoon, was to nourish and nurture their imagination, reason, conscience, and thought life with truth, with the right kind and amounts of nutrients, in order to grow, develop, and fulfill their potential. Doing this on a daily basis develops, in due time, the necessary framework for future success.

Now of course it isn't easy building structure into our lives. Constructing the right kind of framework that is necessary for success. It requires a lot of discipline, determination, and at times self-sacrifice. Sacrificing immediate gratification for future gain, short term desires for long term benefits. But we need to in order to maximize the matter within and without. And it's a lesson that's so hard to learn.

You see, we remember the structure Mom and Dad built into our lives and schedules on the farm. They knew we had to eat right, work hard, rest well and play often in order to develop properly. Our coaches, pastor and teachers knew this too. All of them built into our lives the right kinds and amounts of discipline, challenges and drills that would improve our skills and maximize our talents. And although we didn't like it at times, it was absolutely necessary.

So don't complain and belly ache if you find yourself bouncing around a lot in life, or being used for target practice or as a practice dummy in your Gruntsville experience. All of us at one time or another feels like a rubber egg in Gruntsville, undeveloped, unloved, unfulfilled, uneasy, unequal, unfruitful, unfit, unfinished, unformed, ungodly, unfriendly, and unfortunate. But the good news is you don't have to stay that way. Just focus on feeding your heart, mind and soul a daily, disciplined diet of nourishing news from the trellis of Truth. Like an umbrella or canopy, it will cover, shade, and protect you from Gruntsville's relentless rains of rejection and its ravenous rays of ruin. The trellis of truth will enable you to climb upward and branch outward in your life pursuits. It's a matter of fact. A matter that matters.

TURNING POINTS

In football and hockey it's known as "off-sides"--illegally advancing the ball or puck. And it occurs most often when a player doesn't keep his or her poise.

Jumping off-sides at a critical moment in a game can not only hurt your team, it can become the crucial turning point, the point at which a significant change occurs. It can disrupt concentration and change momentum. It can take a team out of scoring range. And it can lose a game. All because you didn't keep your poise--didn't practice patience under pressure.

I remember the times I jumped off-sides in my life. I remember the time Paterno snuck up behind me and whispered, "I bet you can't block this kick." I was on the maroon platoon practice squad, lined up on the outside of our defense and hungry to make an impression on our coaches by blocking a punt. Of course Paterno's words fueled my fire to block the kick, and in my attempt to get a good jump on the ball, and my coach, I jumped off-sides. Joe just shook his head and walked away. He never said a word, but I knew what he was thinking. He had tested me. He had given me a challenge and I couldn't keep my patience under pressure.

It was a lesson I'll never forget. A real turning point. And I learned from it, even though it was a hard way to learn it. In fact it reminded me of the time I jumped off-sides at home with Mom one morning before school.

I had gone to my closet to get out my favorite outfit to wear because it was "picture day", but it wasn't there. It was still in the wash. So I went straight to Mom and chewed her out for not having it cleaned and ironed.

I didn't have the patience to listen to any of her lame excuses for not having it done, even though I was just one of seven kids in the family getting ready for school that morning, so I just let her have it. And that's when she let me have it. She let me have one of her famous World Heavyweight Boxing backhands. It was sort of like those "Rocky" movies that have slobber and sweat splattering from his mouth and face in slow motion as he gets pummeled with a right hook.

Now I know I should have seen it coming, but I was too busy mouthing off to notice. And after it landed, so did I. I ran down the stairs, (Dad's Wooden Hill), out the door, and up through the field that had been plowed the week before. But I didn't get very far because my feet began to hurt. So I paused for a moment next to the big old oak tree that stood alone in the field to determine the source of my pain. And when I looked down I discovered I was missing some things. I was missing shoes, socks, slacks, and a shirt. There I stood, out in that big open field with nothing but just me and my Fruit Of The Looms.

That's when I landed. When reality kicked in. That's when I came to my senses realizing I had done something very stupid. I had lost my poise. And because I hadn't practiced patience under pressure, I was now standing alone in a big open field wearing nothing but my underwear and a lot of embarrassment.

But things were to get a little worse. With no place to go I turned back to face my Mom and the lesson she held in her hand. She was going to apply her rod of instruction to my seat of understanding. And she did, even though I said and did everything a seventh grader could to get out of it.

But she wanted her lesson to be clearly understood. "Never", she said, "never run away from your problems."

Well she made things clear alright. And I got the point. In fact it was a turning point in my life. An episode that created a significant change in my behavior. A lesson that taught me to throttle back before I got throttled. To practice the attitude and skill of patience under pressure.

What about you?

Are you patient under pressure? Do you practice poise when the pressures of Gruntsville slam hard against your face? Or do you have a tendency to jump off-sides?

Poise can be learned. But you must decide, make up your mind to become a student of it. It is a riser in your staircase to success that must be routinely touched, treaded out in your daily steps of drudgery until it becomes a habit. Until it runs deep in your attitude and actions. And when it becomes rooted in your character you will know it. Because others will see it.

You see, poise in many ways measures a man or woman because it measures depth of character. And depth of character is what pulls people up and through the struggles of Gruntsville.

Unfortunately, too many people are in too great a hurry today to get to their goal. In their pursuit to become successful--to reach the top in a blaze of glory, they jump off-sides. They lose their poise. They lose their sense of balance in life under the stress and strains of the struggle. In auto racing terms they call it, "hitting the wall." Out of control and full throttle, they crash and burn--with nothing but skid marks left behind. All because they measured success by the wrong standards, the wrong dimensions.

Is success measured by how far a man goes? How fast he takes the lead? What kind of car he drives? How much power he has under the hood? What position he has in the race? How many fans he has in the stands? Or how big the headlines are?

Not in the least. None of these things can adequately measure a man or woman because they are the wrong standards. They measure everything but depth of character. They aren't capable of holding a person up and pulling them through when they hit the wall in life.

When the storms strike, when the quake hits, the foundation that keeps them from crumbling--from being blown away--from losing their balance and jumping off-sides, is depth of character.

So consider this lesson as a caution flag. A warning sign to throttle back before you get throttled. Use it as a turning point. An opportunity for change.   S o w the seed of patience in Gruntsville's soil of pressure right now, and then watch it grow into poise as you nurture it along with daily use. It will keep you steady, balanced, under control, and operating on all cylinders as you travel the streets of Gruntsville. It will help you reach the finish line without crashing and burning. And perhaps win you a checkered flag rather than leave you with skidmarks as a legacy.

A WINNING LEGACY

The whole extended family had gathered at the old farm house. Instead of the normal laughter and enthusiasm that marked such gatherings, today there was only low murmuring and drawn faces. Each of us seemed locked in our own world of unattached thoughts, memory flashes and unanswered questions.

Two days earlier, I had received an urgent message at the airport to call my wife, Vicky. Fearing another emergency with our son, Jason, I knew it meant trouble. But I wasn't prepared for the shock that greeted me on the phone. Vicky quietly related the startling message: "It's your Mom, Jeff. She died suddenly at home today."

And now, the day after her funeral, six weeks after winning the Super Bowl, the news still hadn't sunk in. The evidence was there--flowers everywhere, folks coming and going with quiet words of consolation, the tear--stained faces of my brothers and sisters.

But it all seemed so unreal. Any moment now we should hear Mom's familiar call to the supper table, and we'd all gather around to sing our prayer.

We had discovered Mom's diary, and I sat in the family room and opened it. As I did, I left for a moment the present unreality and listened intently once again to the words of the special woman who had helped guide my life.

I pored over page after page of Mom's longings, heartaches, joys, tribulations, convictions. She talked with God on a heart-to-heart basis, as with a trusted friend. Like the Psalmist David, she hid nothing in expressing her innermost emotions and desires.

Mom had known a lot of suffering and sadness in her life. And yet despite family tragedies and a body racked with almost perpetual pain, her faith in God seemed so steadfast. Somehow, even in the darkest moments, Mom knew how to glimpse the pinpoint of God's light in the distance. She clung to His promises with a hope that never quit, and she taught her seven children to do the same.

Every morning as each of us left the house, Mom stitched to our hearts these words: "Remember who you are and Whose you are." And if we ever faced discouragement or confusion, she'd remind us, "God has a very special plan for your life."

How many times, I reflected, did I need to hear those words. Times when it seemed that God had either discarded or forgotten any special plan He might have once had for my life.

As I read Mom's diary, I wondered how it was that no matter what happened, she just kept trusting in God's faithfulness. In every accident, every trial, every disaster Mom somehow saw God's hand of providence.

Like the time I dropped back to pass against the 49'ers, in our National Football Conference Championship Game, that decided which team was going to the Super Bowl. I was focusing on our wide receivers down field, when suddenly, out of the corner of my eye, I glimpsed a flash of red and gold. It was too late. Former Giant-turned-49'er Jim Burt crashed into my leg with the full force of a freight train.

I knew it was over. The pain seared my knee with a vengeance. I dropped to the ground, writhing in pain. I knew right then and there I was finished. In a moment's time, all had been lost.

I turned the page in Mom's diary to where she had been taking notes on that game. Too sick to make the trip to the West Coast, Mom had planted her pained body in front of the television to watch me play. She had made painstaking notes of my statistics, repeated what announcers said about me, and translated her emotions during every key shift in the game. Now, as she watched her son lie on the ground in pain, her diary recorded the depths of her prayers to God.

I'm sure Mom was praying out loud as she wrote. Her words recorded a miracle. In short, emotion-filled sentences, she prayed that God would take away my pain...that He would stoop down and heal her son...and let him finish the game he had waited so many years to play.

Three thousand miles away in San Francisco, I lay on the field while the trainers gathered around me. The pain was brutal.

Suddenly, out of nowhere, everything just stopped. The pain and the fear faded inexplicably. It was unbelievable. I felt a calming, peaceful sensation that started from my head and went down through my leg to my toes.

At the time, I couldn't explain it. One moment I was in total pain, and then all of a sudden I knew everything was okay. I knew I could get up. And I did. A nationwide television audience witnessed what all had said couldn't be done. Our last-minute drive set up a heart-stopping Matt Bahr field goal to win the game and a trip to Super Bowl XXV.

Only when I read Mom's diary did I realize fully what had taken place. I just shook my head in wonder. "I never knew," I mumbled, as tears welled up in my eyes. "I just never knew."

Looking back over the long and difficult road I have traveled, I can now see how God had planned all along to turn trial into triumph.

I can now see how He had never deserted Vick and me, even when He seemed far away in the dark days we spent staring into an incubator. And how He sustained me during those frustrating years in the NFL when it seemed I'd be spending the rest of my career on the sidelines.

I can still hear Mom's words as if she were standing next to me: "You know, son, God has a plan for your life.

Just because things don't go your way doesn't mean the plan has changed."

Like Mom with her tragedies and illnesses, like Dad with his setbacks on the farm, like Jason with his death defying dirge, and like Ron's maroon platoon cocoon, God had allowed trials into my life to forge the inner steel structure of character and faith. I still don't fully understand why certain things have happened in my life; maybe some day I will. But I do know He answers prayer and fulfills the hopes of those who persevere. So my prayer for you is similar to Mom's. When the pain of Gruntsville has you writhing on the ground, may the God of heaven ease your pain, stoop down and restore you, and help you reach your goal and finish the course you have waited so long to run.

Well, we have now come full circle, you and I. From our entrance into Gruntsville, to its exit. We have taken you into the village of our past trials and through its learning gates to a triumphant exit. And as we close out our journey with you, we hope you will learn the lessons we did, as you grope through your own Gruntsville. We hope you'll stitch them to your heart and mind like Mom did to us.

We hope you will listen to the voice of the Gatekeeper. And heed his instruction.

We hope you keep the cabinet of your imagination wide open. Use your council chamber of thought wisely. Tap your treasure of reason daily, and keep the lamp of your conscience burning brightly. Remember, they act as your point man, keeping you on course and moving ahead.

We hope you learn how to bridle your passions, rein in your pride and temper your pursuit of pleasure. Controlling and using them for good, rather than allowing them to control you.

We hope you remember God has a way of getting your attention if you're too busy playing silly games to pass the time. And that Gruntsville is often a wake-up call to get you moving in His direction.

We hope you remember to unlock your vengeful grip of past hurts and hatreds, take a knee, and embrace the transforming power of reconciliation.

We hope you won't be bitten by the poisonous fangs of short cuts. They're a deadend proposition.

We hope you take possession of your time. Use it wisely, and don't worry about things you can't control.

We hope you remember to keep your airways and pathways open and unobstructed while you grope along the streets of Gruntsville. Particularly your airway to heaven. And don't let the noxious fuming frustrations and failures of Gruntsville prevent you from inhaling opportunity, growth, and chance.

We hope you turn your poor, hungry, and driven appetite into a PHD advantage, rather than satiate it with empty entertainment and meaningless, mindless Madison Avenue pursuits.

We hope you will honor God with your body, master the mystery of mind games and pick some dandelions of devotion along the way.

We hope you apply the Noah principle when needed, dominate the dogs of drudgery, use God's smelling salts to restore your spiritual acuity, practice accountability in blood drill, and never forget Tom and Burt.

And most of all, we hope you will leave a lasting legacy as you say goodbye to this world. One that will be remembered and cherished for generations to come.

So get up! Get up like I did when the trials and difficulties of Gruntsville crash into you with the full force of a freight train. Get up, even when the searing pain of Gruntsville is unbearable. And all seems lost.

Remember life is a contact sport. And just because things don't go your way, doesn't mean God's plan for you has changed. In fact, His process of getting you there is just as important as the destination itself. In other words, the journey is just as much a part of His plan as anything else. It's why He allows Gruntsvilles. And if you really think about it, this is the way life is.

From birth to death is one great big Gruntsville experience. And the stages of your life, and the transitions you go through are the gates of your learning experiences, leading to either renewal or ruin.

All along, the God of heaven will whisper instruction, illumine the way, and guide you along according to His plan. He will lead you step by step, little by little until you reach the goal line. A journey that includes both internal and external growth. One that involves the heart, mind, and soul--the invisible, as well as the visible.

And the great thing about the journey is anything can happen, anytime. Great surprises can unfold overnight, in the twinkling of an eye.

This is the legacy Mom left us. And when I say goodbye to this world, I want it to be mine, too. When I am gone, I will have two Super Bowl rings to leave my sons. Perhaps they will remind them of their dad. Of watching him play on those glorious Sunday afternoons. But what I want them to remember most, is not so much my statistics, or even my Super Bowl win, but the story behind them. The chapters on perseverance, commitment, hard work, failure, hope, despair, suffering, team work, family, love, passion, preparation, humility, courage, toughness, and especially character and faith. This is the inside stuff I want to stitch into their heart, mind, and soul. Because this is the stuff winning legacies are made of.

You see, when I am gone, what I leave IN my children will be far more important to me than what I leave FOR them.

So get up! Dig in and come back when Gruntsville has you down and out. If "62 come-back dig" can work in a Super Bowl, it can work in your life. When I looked into the faces of those ten men to call that play, they were the sweaty, determined faces of ten men who had come to win. And I hope you're wearing that same sweaty, determined look right now. I hope you have come to win.

So don't sit in the corner and pout, feeling sorry for yourself. Or allow the bumps and bruises of the journey to keep you from fulfilling your purpose and reaching your goal. Get back in the game. You have lessons to learn, a Gruntsville to conquer, and a winning legacy to leave. So get up. You can make it. If you don't, you will never know what could have been.

Don't lose heart in doing good,
for in due time you shall reap,
if you don't quit.
Ron Hostetler

Ron Hostetler

Ron grew up in rural Pennsylvania as the oldest boy of seven children in a Mennonite farming family. Their parents and church encouraged them to develop a personal faith in God, a solid work ethic, and a commitment to the family.

As co-captain of the Penn State football team, Ron was named All-East and preseason All-American and Sports Illustrated Defensive Player of the Week. One of his end zone interceptions even showed up in Hollywood in a scene from the movie, "Lethal Weapon." After the Los Angeles Rams drafted him for the NFL, Ron cut short his professional career due to a debilitating knee injury.

Ron earned the B.S. degree from Penn State, and his Masters Degree equivalency there and at Millersville University in behavioral science and clinical psychology. He teaches at the Milton Hershey School, a private residential school for financially needy and orphan children, and has coached at all interscholastic levels.

Ron is an active member of a local church, President of the Derry Township School Board of Directors, and founder and Chairman of the Board of Family Impact, a non profit organization dedicated to strengthening families.

Much in demand as a motivational speaker, Ron has encouraged many to cultivate their dreams, to persevere in times of trouble, and to realize their God-given potential. He has traveled to South America and throughout the United States speaking to fathers and sons, athletes and businessmen, conventions and organizations.

Ron and his wife Holly, who also serves with Family Impact, have four children. Together, the Hostetlers conduct seminars and workshops and perform in song for churches, schools, and business and civic groups. Contact Family Impact if you are interested in receiving the Family Impact newsletter, scheduling an event, or contacting Ron and Holly: Family Impact • 24 Tice Avenue • Hershey, Pennsylvania • 17033 • (717) 533-8349

139